SEPHARIAL'S ASTROLOGY

HOW TO MAKE AND READ YOUR OWN HOROSCOPE

Contents: The Alphabet of the Heavens; The Construction of a Horoscope; How to Read a Horoscope; The Stars in their Courses.

Sepharial

ISBN 1-56459-819-5

Request our FREE CATALOG of over 1,000

Rare Esoteric Books

Unavailable Elsewhere

Alchemy, Ancient Wisdom, Astronomy, Baconian, Eastern-Thought, Egyptology, Esoteric, Freemasonry, Gnosticism, Hermetic, Magic, Metaphysics, Mysticism, Mystery Schools, Mythology, Occult, Philosophy, Psychology, Pyramids, Qabalah, Religions, Rosicrucian, Science, Spiritual, Symbolism, Tarot, Theosophy, *and many more!*

Kessinger Publishing Company
Montana, U.S.A.

Introduction

FROM the earliest ages of the world's history the subject of Astrology has excited the interest of, and exercised a great influence over, the minds of a certain order of thinking men. The science has never been universal in its acceptance, though it is safe to say that, with its countless adherents in the East and the ever-increasing number of its advocates in the West, there is no faith which has a more universal application than the belief in the influence of the heavenly bodies over the destinies of human beings. It is not possible within the limits of a small handbook such as this to adequately consider the philosophic paradox which makes of Freewill in man a "necessity in play"; but it is obvious that the concept is not altogether unscientific, seeing that it is customary to speak of the "free path of vibration" in chemical atoms while at the same time it is known that these atoms have their restricted characteristics, modes of motion, &c., and are all subject to the general laws controlling the bodies of which they form integral parts. Let it suffice that if we can trace an actual connectedness between the disposition of the heavenly bodies at the moment of a birth and the known life and character of the individual then born, and an exact correspondence

Introduction

between the course of events in that life with the changes occurring in the heavens subsequent to the moment of birth, we shall do well to accept the fact for what it is worth, and arrange our philosophic notions accordingly.

As far back as the year B. C. 2154, we find mention of the great importance attaching to the celestial phenomena in the minds of Chinese rulers. It is recorded in the Historical Classic of China that at that time the astrologers Hi and Ho neglected their duties so that when, on the 10th of October, there was a great eclipse of the Sun at Peking between seven and nine o'clock in the morning, the people were wholly unprepared for it, and "ran about here and there in the utmost consternation." For this offence Hi and Ho were deprived of their offices, their estates were confiscated and they were driven from the kingdom. Among the Hindus we have the classical writers Garga, Parashara, and Mihira, together with their legions of commentators. The Assyrian records are full of astrological allusions regarding the influence of planetary conjunctions and stellar positions. The Greek mythology is nothing but a vast system of cosmographical astrology, and there is no other history in it than what you may read in the constellations of the heavens and the corresponding evolution of the human race. Aristotle made it a part of his philosophy. Hipparchus, Hippocrates, Thales, Galenius, and others subscribed an intelligent belief in its principles. To Claudius Ptolemy, however, we are indebted for the first concise and scientific statement of its principles and practice, so far as Europe is concerned. He wrote the Tetrabiblos, or Four Books, and laid the foundations of

Introduction

a true astrological science. Julius Firmicus confirmed Ptolemy and enlarged upon his observations. The subsequent discovery of the planets Uranus and Neptune by Herschel and Adams, widened the field of research and gave to later astrologers the clue to much that hitherto had been imperfectly understood. Not that these discoveries overturned the whole system of astrology, as some have imagined and foolishly stated, or that they negatived the conclusions drawn from the observed effects of the seven anciently known bodies of the solar system, but it became possible after a lapse of time to fill in the blank spaces and to account for certain events which had not been traced to the action of any of the already known planets. The discovery of argon did not destroy our conclusions regarding the nature and characteristics of oxygen or hydrogen or nitrogen, nor give an entirely new meaning to the word "atmosphere." If even so many as seven new planets should be discovered, there would yet not be a single paragraph of this book which would need revising. What is known regarding planetary action in human life is known with great certainty, and the effects of one planet can never be confounded with those of another. Incomplete as it must needs be, it is yet a veritable science both as to its principles and practice. It claims for itself a place among the sciences for the sole reason that it is capable of mathematical demonstration, and deals only with the observed positions and motions of the heavenly bodies; and the man who holds to the principia of Newton, the solidarity of the solar system, the interaction of the planetary bodies and their consequent electrostatic effects upon the Earth, cannot, while subject to the air he

Introduction

breathes, deny the foundation principles of astrology. The application of these principles to the facts of everyday life is solely a matter of prolonged research and tabulation upon an elaborate scale which has been going on for thousands of years in all parts of the world, so that all the reader has to do is to make his own horoscope and put the science to the test of true or false. The present writer is in a position to know that the study of astrology at the present day is no less sincere than widely spread, but few care to let their studies be known, for, as Prof. F. Max Müller recently said, "So great is the ignorance which confounds a science requiring the highest education, with that of the ordinary gipsy fortune-teller." That to which the great Kepler was compelled "by his unfailing experience of the course of events in harmony with the changes taking place in the heavens," to subscribe "an unwilling belief," the science which was practised and advocated by Tycho Brahe under all assaults of fortune and adverse opinion, the art that arrested the attention of the young Newton and set him pondering upon the problems of force and matter, which fascinated the minds of such men as Francis Bacon, Archbishop Usher, Haley, Sir George Witchell, Flamstead, and a host of others, is to-day the favorite theme of thousands of intelligent minds and bids fair to become a subject of popular inquiry.

It is believed that the present work will be of considerable assistance to those who seriously contemplate an initial study of the science of horoscopy, and although it by no means exhausts what is known on the subject, yet it will be found accurate and reliable as far as it goes, and will enable any one of ordinary intelligence to test

Introduction

the claims of Astrology for himself. This is as much as can be expected in the limits of a small handbook. The literature of the subject is considerable, and the present writer only takes credit to himself so far as his own wide experience and practice have enabled him to present the subject in a simple and brief manner.

Contents

SECTION I

THE ALPHABET OF THE HEAVENS

CHAP.   PAGE

I. The Planets, Their Natures and Types............. 17
II. The Signs of the Zodiac......................... 24
III. The Celestial Houses........................... 29
IV. The Astronomical Aspects....................... 31

SECTION II

THE CONSTRUCTION OF A HOROSCOPE

I. The Ephemeris and Its Uses...................... 34
II. To Erect a Figure of the Heavens................ 36
III. The Tables of Houses........................... 39
IV. Planetary Transits.............................. 43
V. Table of Eclipses................................ 47

SECTION III

HOW TO READ THE HOROSCOPE

I. The Planets in the Houses....................... 51
II. The Constitution................................ 54
III. Health and Sickness............................ 56
IV. How to Read Character and Disposition.......... 59

Contents

CHAP.		PAGE
V.	Financial Prospects	64
VI.	The Position in Life	69
VII.	The Choice of Occupation	72
VIII.	Marriage Circumstances	76
IX.	Indications of Progeny	81
X.	Voyages and Journeys	84
XI.	Of Friends and Enemies	87
XII.	The End of Life	91

SECTION IV

THE STARS IN THEIR COURSES

I.	The Time-measure	94
II.	The Effects of Transits	101
III.	How to Summarise a Horoscope	105
IV.	How to Become a Successful Astrologer	108
V.	A Popular Illustration	114

Astrology

SECTION I

THE ALPHABET OF THE HEAVENS

CHAPTER I

THE PLANETS, THEIR NATURES AND TYPES

THE luminaries and planets are known to astronomers under the following names and symbols:

The Sun ☉, Moon ☽, Neptune ♆, Uranus ♅, Saturn ♄, Jupiter ♃, Mars ♂, Venus ♀, and Mercury ☿.

Neptune revolves around the Sun in its distant orbit once in about 165 years. Uranus completes its orbital revolution in 84 years, Jupiter in 12 years, Mars in about 15 months, Venus in 11 months, and Mercury in 18 weeks. If you imagine these bodies to be revolving in a plane around the Sun and yourself to be standing within the Sun, the motions of these bodies will appear almost uniform and always in one direction. Were the orbits of the planets circular and the Sun holding the centre of the circle, their motions would be constant, that is to say, always in the same direction and at the same rate. But the orbits are elliptical, and the Sun holds a position in one of the foci of each ellipse. Consequently the planets are at times further from the Sun than at others, and they are then said to be

Astrology

in their aphelion, the opposite point of the orbit where they are nearest to the Sun being called the perihelion. When at aphelion the planets move slower, and when at perihelion they move quicker than at the mean distance. Astronomers employ an imaginary circular orbit for the planets, in which they move at an uniform rate of velocity, which is called the mean motion. This is subject to an equation depending on the position of the planet in its orbit, and it determines the difference between the imaginary planet and the true planet. The equation itself depends on the eccentricity of the orbit, that is to say, its relation to a circle drawn around the same focal centre. The Earth follows the same laws as all other bodies of the same system.

But if we imagine the Earth to be stationary in space and the centre around which the planets revolve, their motions present several irregularities. Mercury and Venus will then appear to revolve around the Sun while the Sun revolves around the Earth, sometimes being between the Earth and the Sun, which is called an Inferior conjunction, sometimes on the further side of the Sun away from the Earth, as at their Superior conjunction; and again, at other times to the right or left of the Sun, in East or West elongation. The other planets, having orbits greater than that of the Earth, will appear to revolve around it at constantly varying distances and velocities. At certain points in their orbits they will appear to remain stationary in the same part of the Zodiac. The annexed illustration will assist the lay reader perhaps. The body M is Mercury when at Inferior conjunction with the Sun, as seen from the Earth. The letter V is the planet Venus at Superior

Planets, their Natures and Types

conjunction with the Sun. The points W and E are the points of greatest elongation West and East, and the letter S shows the points in the orbit at which those bodies appear to be stationary when viewed from the Earth, at G. As seen from the Earth, Venus would appear to be direct and Mercury retrograde.

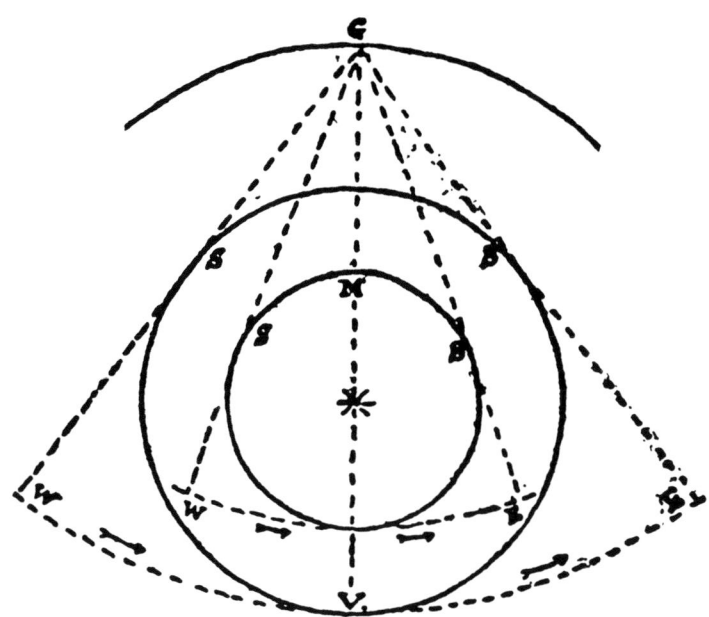

Astrologically we regard the Earth as the passive subject of planetary influence, and we have therefore to regard it as the centre of the field of activity. If we were making a horoscope for an inhabitant of the planet Mars, we should make Mars the centre of the system. The planets' positions are therefore taken as from the centre of the Earth (Geocentric), and not as from the centre of the Sun (Heliocentric). An astrological Ephemeris of the planets' motions is em-

Astrology

ployed for this purpose (see Sect. II., chap. i.), and there are 480,000 of these sold to astrologers or students of astrology every year, from which fact it is possible to draw one's own conclusions as to the state of Astrology in the West. These figures, of course, do not include the millions of almanac readers nor the Oriental students, who prepare their own ephemerides.

Knowing the simple natures of the several planets we are able to arrive at an estimate of their effects when acting in combination.

Neptune acts upon the mind of man to produce a highly-strung nervous temperament, often allied to either insanity or genius; neurosis, aphasia, &c. It produces complications in business and an involved state of affairs generally. Disposes to fraud, double-dealing, and irresponsible actions. In the body it produces waste of tissue and a consumptive habit.

Uranus gives an eccentric mind, waywardness, originality, inventiveness. Acting on the affairs of business, it produces sudden and unexpected developments, irregularities, rapid rise and fall, instability, unexpected turns of good and bad fortune. In the body it has relation to the nervous system, and its diseases are those of paralysis, lesion, and nervous derangement.

Saturn produces a thoughtful, sober, ponderable mind; steadfastness, patience, and endurance; disposition to routine and habit, method. In financial affairs it gives steady results commensurate with labor, success that is slow but sure, durance, hardships, privations. In the body it is related to the osseous system, and its effects are brought about by obstructions, chills, and inhibition of function.

Planets, their Natures and Types

Jupiter gives joviality, optimism, bountifulness, generosity, a rich and fruitful mind. It renders the subject fortunate in his affairs, giving success and frequently opulence. With this planet strong in the horoscope a person never "goes under." In the body it has relation to the arterial process, and its diseases are those which arise from surfeit, congestion, and plethora.

Mars confers a sense of freedom, much ambition and executive ability, frankness, truthfulness, and scorn of consequence. It renders the mind forceful and militant, stimulates to new projects and enterprises, and in the body of man has relation to the muscular system. Its diseases are those which arise from inflammatory action in the tissues.

Venus confers poesy, good taste, fine feeling, artistic powers, gentleness, docility, dalliance, and love of pleasure. It renders the affairs pleasant and prosperous, giving profit from both artistic and rustic pursuits. Next to Jupiter it is the most benefic of the planets in its action on mankind. In the body it has relation to the venous system, and its diseases are those which arise from impurities of the blood, scorbutic and zymotic diseases, eczema, smallpox, measles, &c.

Mercury renders its subjects active, versatile, apt and business-like, disposed to much commerce, whether of the mind or the market, and eager in the pursuit of knowledge; alert, and well-informed. Its influence on affairs of life is variable, for it always translates the nature of that planet to which at birth it is in nearest aspect (Sect. I., chap. iv.). In the body it is related to the sensorium, the centres of sensation, and reflexly controls the nerves of action.

Astrology

The Moon gives gracefulness of manner and suavity of speech, softness and adaptability of nature, variableness, love of change, romance, and adventure; disposed to exploration and voyaging. In the body it corresponds to the glandular system, and its diseases are those incidental to the lymphatic glands and vascular tissue.

The Sun renders its subjects magnanimous, noble, proud, despising all mean and sordid actions; loyal, truthful, and fearless. It produces honors and the favor of dignitaries, and renders the subject fortunate in the control of his affairs. In the body it controls the vital principle.

The types of persons produced by the various planets are very distinct, the chief features of each being as follows:

Neptune—Thin, nervous-looking people, blue eyes, soft, silky hair, thin and usually long faces, frequently wearing a strained or startled look. *Uranus*—Tall, wiry, and energetic figures, alert, muscular, spasmodic, and with some touch of eccentricity. *Saturn*—Dark and lean people, small, deep-set eyes, heavy brows, long noses, thin lips, and sallow complexions. *Jupiter*—Full-bodied, robust men, large and expressive blue or brown eyes, arched brows, high foreheads, oval faces, and rich brown hair. *Mars*—Strong, muscular, and athletic bodies, ruddy complexion, grey eyes, prominent brows, sloping forehead, and usually some mark or scar in the face. *Sun*—Fresh, clear complexion, blue or grey eyes, round head, broad shoulders, strong jaws, upright and dignified carriage. *Venus*—Elegant, well-groomed, and often dainty-looking people, with blue or soft brown eyes, brown hair, fine teeth and finger-nails, small feet

Planets, their Natures and Types

and short fleshy hands. *Mercury*—Thin, tall, and active bodies, alert appearance, small and usually dark eyes; wide, thin lips, long arms and slender hands. Frequently great talkers and quick walkers. *Moon*—Rather short and fleshy people, with pale face, soft limpid eyes, sad brown or medium colored hair, fine teeth, broad chest, and a tendency to a squat fulness of body. The forehead is usually high and broad.

Look at the people as they pass you in the street. Bring them if possible under one or other of these types. Consider what has been said of the planets' natures, and you have a ready key to something of their character and destiny.

CHAPTER II

THE SIGNS OF THE ZODIAC

THE Zodiac is an imaginary belt of the Heavens through which the Sun and planets move in their apparent revolutions round the Earth. It extends from 23° 27' above the plane of the Equator to the same distance below it, being bounded by the Tropic of Cancer on the North and by that of Capricorn on the South. The Ecliptic is a circle transecting this belt at an angle of 23° 27' to the plane of the Equator. The points where it cuts the Equator are called the Equinoxes.

The Ecliptic is divided into twelve equal sections, counting from the Vernal Equinox. These are called the Signs of the Zodiac. Each sign occupies 30 degrees of the circle.

Their names and symbols are as follows:—

1. Aries, the Ram	♈	7. Libra, the Balance	♎
2. Taurus, the Bull	♉	8. Scorpio, the Scorpion	♏
3. Gemini, the Twins	♊	9. Sagittarius, the Hunter	♐
4. Cancer, the Crab	♋	10. Capricornus, the Goat	♑
5. Leo, the Lion	♌	11. Aquarius, the Waterman	♒
6. Virgo, the Virgin	♍	12. Pisces, the Fishes	♓

The Signs of the Zodiac

For Astrological purposes they are grouped according to the element and the constitution which they represent, thus:—

ELEMENTS.

Fire—Aries, Leo, Sagittarius.
Earth—Taurus, Virgo, Capricornus.
Air—Gemini, Libra, Aquarius.
Water—Cancer, Scorpio, Pisces.

CONSTITUTIONS.

Movable—Aries, Cancer, Libra, Capricornus.
Fixed—Taurus, Leo, Scorpio, Aquarius.
Flexed—Gemini, Virgo, Sagittarius, Pisces.

Every alternate sign, beginning with Aries, is male, and the rest are female. Aries, male; Taurus, female; Gemini, male; Cancer, female, &c. The signs Aries, Leo, Capricornus are called barren, while Taurus, Cancer, Scorpio, and Pisces are fruitful. Aries governs the East, Cancer the North, Libra the West, and Capricornus the South.

The Double-bodied signs are Gemini, Sagittarius, and Pisces. It is important that all these classifications should be learned, as they form an essential part of the doctrine of Astrology, and are frequently employed in the reading of a Horoscope.

The types of people under the various signs should also be known as intimately as possible. A person is said to be "under" a sign—that is to say, under its influence, when that sign is rising in the East at the

Astrology

moment of birth. You will recognise these types among your friends and associates:—

Aries produces a person of lean body, long neck, high cheek-bones, grey eyes, sandy or sad brown hair, which is either wiry and straight or crisp and curling. The front teeth are usually large and prominent.

Taurus gives a full, thick-set body, strong neck and shoulders, full brown eyes, dark curling hair, full lips, rather wide mouth, and round, bullet-shaped head. The hands and feet are short and fleshy.

Gemini produces a tall, active, and upright body, long arms and legs, wide, thin lips, straight and often *retroussé* nose, lank, straight black hair, rather wide shoulders, and thin body.

Cancer denotes a rather short, squat figure, full lymphatic body, pale complexion, round face, broad forehead, sad brown hair, large aqueous eyes, full chest, short, fleshy hands and feet.

Leo renders its subjects tall, broad shouldered, fine and manly figures, small round head, fair complexion, blue or grey eyes, flaxen or fair brown hair, upright and fearless carriage.

Virgo renders the body thin and active, the head well developed, the forehead broad, hair light brown and waving off the forehead, eyes blue, shoulders broad, the type being of an intellectual or artistic form.

Libra gives an elegant body, well-developed limbs, fine oval face, straight nose, fine blue eyes (sometimes deep brown), flaxen or chestnut hair, beautiful complexion. The highest types of beauty are to be found under this sign.

Scorpio gives a short, thick-set, and powerful figure,

The Signs of the Zodiac

broad, deep chest, dusky or sallow complexion, dark curling or crisp hair, strong and rather bowed legs. This is a very virile and robust type.

Sagittarius gives a tall person, well-made figure, elegant limbs, oval and rather long face, brown or chestnut hair growing off the forehead, fine expressive eyes, rather prominent and of a dark brown or blue color, long nose, slightly aquiline.

Capricornus produces a slight and rather ill-formed person, long and scraggy neck, prominent features, narrow chin, weak and frequently decrepit limbs, weak chest and sloping shoulders. Frequently the figure is wiry and suggestive of considerable powers of endurance. The brows are prominent, the nose long, and the face thin and hard-set.

Aquarius contributes the finest types of beauty next to Libra. The Saxon type is dominant. A tall figure, well formed and rounded, fair complexion and blue eyes, flaxen hair, straight features, well-developed chin, and fine, clear forehead.

Pisces produces one of rather short stature, short limbs, lymphatic body, pale complexion, limpid blue eyes, black or brown eyes, short nose, full lips, round face, small hands and feet.

The short signs are Taurus, Cancer, Capricornus, and Pisces. The tall signs are Gemini, Leo, Sagittarius, and Aquarius. The others are of medium height.

The planets rising in each sign will always alter the type by impressing their own characteristics on the subject.

Each sign has a Ruler, and the position of the ruler of the rising sign has much to do with the physical confor-

Astrology

mation, as if Taurus be rising and Venus, its ruler, be in Leo, the person will be taller and fairer than indicated by Taurus alone. Pure types are very uncommon.

The rulership of the planets in the signs is as follows:—

> Saturn governs Aquarius and Capricornus.
> Jupiter governs Pisces and Sagittarius.
> Mars governs Aries and Scorpio.
> Venus governs Taurus and Libra.
> Mercury governs Gemini and Virgo.
> The Moon governs Cancer, and Leo is governed by the Sun.

When a planet is found in a sign over which it is said to govern it acts more strongly than usual, and when in the opposite signs to those it governs it is said to be in its "fall," when it is weaker than usual.

Planets governing opposite signs to one another are said to be "enemies." Such do not produce harmonious and favorable results when acting in conjunction.

CHAPTER III

THE CELESTIAL HOUSES

THE imaginary circle which passes immediately over your head as you face the South is called the Prime Vertical. This is divided for astrological purposes into twelve equal divisions called Houses, six of which are above the horizon and six below it. They are counted from the East Horizon under the Earth to the West, and thence through the zenith to the East again. The figure in Section IV., chapter v., will make the idea easy of comprehension.

Each such division or House carries its own signification, and it has been ascertained beyond all doubt or cavil that the ruling of the Ancients in this matter is altogether reliable, however empirical it may appear.

The First House governs the personal appearance, but chiefly the face and head. The Second House rules over finance, movable effects, commerce. In the body it governs the neck and throat. The Third House governs short journeys, letters, and other means of communication, near relations or neighbors. In the body it governs the arms and lungs. The Fourth House governs real estate, the residence, the produce of the earth, the mother

Astrology

of the subject, and the end of life. In the body, the breasts and thorax. The Fifth House governs progeny, the sex instincts, domestic relations, and social pleasures. In the body, the back and heart. The Sixth House governs the health, servants, and personal comforts of the subject, clothes, food, and other physical requisites, sanitation, hygiene. In the body it rules over the abdomen and lower viscera. The Seventh House has dominion over marriage, contracts, agreements, partners, and matters of exchange. In the body it has relation to the loins and kidneys. The Eighth House rules death, loss, legacies and dowries, and matters appertaining to the deceased. In the body it is related to the excretory system. The Ninth House is said to govern long journeys, publications, religious beliefs, foreign lands, and legal affairs. In the body it rules the thighs. The Tenth House rules over position, honor and fame of the subject, the father, superiors of all orders. In the body it rules over the knees. The Eleventh House governs friends, social relations, societies and companies with which the subject is concerned. In the body it has relation to the legs from calf to ankle. The Twelfth House rules ambushes, restraints, privations, imprisonments, confinements, and all limitations of the personal freedom. In the body it rules the ankles and feet.

Applying these significations to the interpretation of a horoscope it will be seen that if Mars should be rising at the moment of birth there will be a scar or mark on the face. Observations of this sort will frequently assist to determine the time of birth when it is not known. Similarly with other planets in the same or other Houses; but of this more anon.

CHAPTER IV

THE ASTRONOMICAL ASPECTS

ASPECTS are certain angular distances measured on the Ecliptic, and they form a fundamental part of astrological science. Any planet may be good or bad in its effects on the character and destiny, according to the aspect that it throws to the chief points of the Horoscope. The aspects are: The semisquare aspect of 45 degrees, sextile of 60 degrees, square of 90 degrees, trine of 120 degrees, sesquiquadrate of 135 degrees, and the opposition of 180 degrees. There is also the conjunction, when bodies are in the same degree or part of a Sign.

The good aspects are the trine and sextile; the evil being the semisquare, square, sesquiquadrate, and opposition. The aspect of a planet determines its effects, whether for good or evil. The conjunction is good with good planets, such as Jupiter and Venus, and evil with malefic planets such as Mars and Saturn.

When planets are the same distance North or South of the Equator they are in parallel declination (p.d.), and they then act as if in conjunction. Also when planets are in mutual disposition, that is to say, occupying one another's signs, they act as if they were in conjunction.

Astrology

Planets in conjunction act according to their simple natures, but when in aspect, according to the nature of that aspect. The benefic planets Jupiter, Venus, Sun, Moon, and also Mercury when in good disposition with another planet or in a congenial Sign, produce good effects by their conjunctions and by their trine and sextile aspects; but when in square, semisquare, or sesquisquare aspect they are uniformly evil in effect. On the other hand, the malefic planets Neptune, Uranus, Saturn, and Mars, together with Mercury when ill-disposed or in uncongenial Signs, are evil in their effects when in conjunction with the significant points of the horoscope; also when in evil aspect; but they nevertheless produce good effects when in good aspect.

The Significators

The more important points of the Horoscope to which aspect can be thrown are called "Significators." The general significators in any horoscope are the Sun, the Moon, the Midheaven (the degree which holds the meridian of the horoscope), and the Ascendant (the degree which is rising). But every planet can be a particular significator in its own province, namely, in the Sign which it rules, and the House in which it is found at birth.

In a general sense the Moon is significant of the mother, female relations, the personal health and fortunes and the changes incident to these. The Sun in the same way indicates the father, male relations, the vital principle, and position. Mercury is the significator of the mind and intellect, the faculties generally. Venus is significatrix of love affairs, domestic relations, pleasures, and of

The Astronomical Aspects

young female relations, sisters, &c. Mars is significator of enterprises, strifes, and young male relations. Jupiter is significator of increase and emoluments; Saturn of legacies, inheritance, and aged persons; Uranus of civic and governmental bodies; Neptune of voyages and psychic experiences. The chief points to be regarded, however, are the Midheaven, the Ascendant, and the places of the Sun and Moon.

SECTION II

THE CONSTRUCTION OF A HOROSCOPE

CHAPTER I

THE EPHEMERIS AND ITS USES

An Ephemeris is an almanac of the planetary positions day by day throughout any given year. They are to be obtained at a small cost, in a convenient form specially adapted to the use of astrologers. In the first column will be found the Sidereal Time for the day, which is the Sun's Right Ascension or distance from the Vernal Equinox, expressed in Hours, Minutes, and Seconds, and equated to Mean Time at Greenwich. By merely adding the time after noon, or subtracting the hours and minutes before noon, at which the birth took place, you will obtain the Right Ascension of the Mid-heaven at the moment of birth. The use to which this is put will appear in the next chapter. It corresponds to a particular degree of the Zodiac which is in the Mid-heaven at the given time of birth.

The next column contains the Sun's longitude at Noon for each day. By taking the position on one day from

The Ephemeris and its Uses

that on the next day, the motion of the Sun for 24 hours is obtained, and a proportion of this for the hour of birth can easily be made. The mean motion of the Sun per day is 2½', or 1 degree per day. In another column will be found the Moon's longitude, and in adjacent columns its declination and latitude. Declination is distance North or South of the Equator, and celestial latitude is distance North or South of the Ecliptic. The longitudes of the other bodies are also given for each day at noon.

The mean longitudinal progress of the several bodies is as follows: Sun, 2½' per hour, or 1 degree per day; Moon, 32' per hour, or 13 degrees per day; Neptune, 2' per day; Uranus, 3' per day; Saturn, about 5' per day; Jupiter, about 12' per day; Mars, 45' per day, or about 2' per hour; Venus, 72' per day, or 3' per hour; Mercury, 84' per day, or 3½' per hour. These increments are for direct motion only; the planets are, as already explained, sometimes retrograde and sometimes stationary. The Horoscope of birth is only concerned with the longitudes of the planets, but when one or more planets have the same declination North or South, they should be noted as being in Parallel, for they then act as if they were in conjunction.

Take in hand, then, the Ephemeris for the year of your birth and read this chapter with it in view. After understanding its construction, extract the Sidereal Time at Noon for the day of your birth and refer to the next chapter.

CHAPTER II

TO ERECT A FIGURE OF THE HEAVENS

TAKE the Sidereal time at noon on the day of birth, and add to it the hours and minutes after noon at which you were born, or if before noon, subtract from it the interval between the birth and noon. This will give the approximate Right Ascension of the Midheaven at birth. Thus, suppose a person to be born on May 1, 1890, at 3h. 30m. p.m. in London—

The Sidereal time, noon, May 1, 1890, is..2h. 36m. 28s.
To which add time p.m.................3   30   0
Acceleration at 10″ per hour...........0   0   34
Right Ascension of Midheaven at Birth....6h. 7m. 2s.

With this Right Ascension of the Midheaven you then refer to Tables of Houses for London (see Chapter III.), and against this quantity of Sidereal Time you will find, under the column marked 10, the sign and degree which corresponds to it, namely, the 2nd of Cancer. This is put at the head of the figure, and the rest of the signs are placed around the figure in their order as shown in the Table. Only six of the Houses are given in the

To Erect a Figure of the Heavens

Tables, because the opposite Houses will have the *same* degrees of the *opposite* signs on them. Thus we read against the Right Ascension 6h. 7m. 28s. the following:—

| 10 | 11 | 12 | Ascen. | 2 | 3 |

Cancer 2, Leo 8, Virgo 8, Libra 1.33, Libra 26, Scorp. 26.

This means that the 2nd degree of Cancer was on the cusp of the Tenth House (the Midheaven) at the moment of the birth, Leo 8th on the cusp of the Eleventh House, Virgo 8th on the cusp of the Twelfth, Libra 1.33 on the Ascendant or Eastern Horizon, and so of the rest. On the cusp of the Fourth House we place Capricornus 2, because the Fourth House is opposite the 10th and the sign Capricornus is opposite to Cancer. On the cusp of the Fifth House we place Aquarius 8, because the Fifth House is opposite to the Eleventh, and Aquarius is opposite to Leo. When completed we find the cusps of the Houses as follows, opposite to those in the Tables:—

| 4 | 5 | 6 | 7 | 8 | 9 |

Capric. 2, Aquar. 8, Pisces 8, Aries 1.33, Aries 26, Taur. 26.

It is then only necessary to place the planets in the figure, as explained in the preceding chapter, and the figure of the Heavens is complete.

To Draw a Figure of the Heavens

Take a pair of compasses, and with a radius of about 2½ inches, describe a circle. Within this, and with a radius of about 2 inches, describe another. With the radius of this latter mark off six equal divisions, and then

Astrology

equally divide these so as to make twelve. Within the figure draw a small circle, concentric with the others, to represent the Earth. From the points of division already obtained draw straight lines to the centre of the figure until they touch the circle of the Earth. You then have a figure which represents the Houses of the Heavens, being a twelvefold division of the Prime Vertical. The lines extending from the outer circles to the Earth are the cusps of the Houses (see fig. Section IV., chap. 5).

The degrees of the Zodiac which are upon the cusps of the Houses, as found in the Tables opposite a given Sidereal Time, are written over the several cusps in their order between the two outer circles. Reference to the Ephemeris for May 1, 1890, shows the Sun at noon in Taurus 11 degrees 2 minutes. Three and a half hours later it will have advanced about 8 minutes in longitude, so that its position will be in Taurus 11 degrees 10 minutes. This longitude falls in the Eighth House, and we therefore place the symbol of the Sun in that division of the Heavens and place against it the figures 11.10, so that as Aries 26 is on the cusp of the Eighth and Taurus 26 on the cusp of the Ninth House, the Sun's position in Taurus 11.10 will fall between these cusps, *i. e.*, in the Eighth House. The rest of the planets are placed in the figure according to their respective longitudes.

CHAPTER III

THE TABLES OF HOUSES

The Tables of the Houses on pp. 40, 41, are calculated for the latitude of 51° 32' North. This will serve for London and environs, and approximately for the South of England and the Midlands. A useful set of tables of Houses for other latitudes may be obtained through the booksellers.

In order to illustrate the uses to which these Tables may be put in the solution of astronomical problems, let us take the Sun's position in the horoscope for the 1st of May, 1890, and find when the Sun sets on that day on the horizon of London. The Sun sets on Taurus, 11 degrees, and it will set when the opposite point of the Heavens is rising. Find under the column marked "Ascen." the 11th degree of Scorpio, and against it in the column marked "Sidereal Time" you will find 9h. 49m. 9s. This will be the Right Ascension of the Midheaven when the Sun sets on London. We have already seen that the Sidereal Time at noon on the 1st of May was 2h. 37m. 28s., and this, taken from the former Sidereal Time, gives about 7.12 p.m. as the time of sunset. Now in the example horoscope the birth took place at 3.30 p.m., and this time, taken from 7.12 p.m., gives 3h. 42m. from birth to sunset. If you multiply this by

Sidereal Time. H.	M.	S.	10 ♎ °	11 ♎ °	12 ♏ °	Ascen ♐ °	'	2 ♑ °	3 ♒ °
12	0	0	0	27	17	3	23	8	21
12	3	40	1	28	18	4	4	9	22
12	7	20	2	29	19	4	45	10	24
12	11	0	3	♏	20	5	26	11	25
12	14	41	4	1	20	6	7	12	26
12	18	21	5	1	21	6	48	13	27
12	22	2	6	2	22	7	29	14	28
12	25	42	7	3	23	8	10	15	29
12	29	23	8	4	23	8	51	16	♓
12	33	4	9	5	24	9	33	17	2
12	36	45	10	6	25	10	15	18	3
12	40	26	11	6	25	10	57	19	4
12	44	8	12	7	26	11	40	20	5
12	47	50	13	8	27	12	22	21	6
12	51	32	14	9	28	13	4	22	7
12	55	14	15	10	28	13	47	23	9
12	58	57	16	11	29	14	30	24	10
13	2	40	17	11	♐	15	14	25	11
13	6	23	18	12	1	15	59	26	12
13	10	7	19	13	1	16	44	27	13
13	13	51	20	14	2	17	29	28	15
13	17	35	21	15	3	18	14	29	16
13	21	20	22	16	4	19	0	♒	17
13	25	6	23	16	4	19	45	1	18
13	28	52	24	17	5	20	31	2	20
13	32	38	25	18	6	21	18	4	21
13	36	25	26	19	7	22	6	5	22
13	40	12	27	20	7	22	54	6	23
13	44	0	28	21	8	23	42	7	25
13	47	48	29	21	9	24	31	8	26
13	51	37	30	22	10	25	20	10	27

Sidereal Time. H.	M.	S.	10 ♏ °	11 ♏ °	12 ♐ °	Ascen ♐ °	'	2 ♒ °	3 ♓ °
13	51	37	0	22	10	25	20	10	27
13	55	27	1	23	11	26	10	11	28
13	59	17	2	24	11	27	2	12	♈
14	3	8	3	25	12	27	53	14	1
14	6	59	4	26	13	28	45	15	2
14	10	51	5	26	14	29	36	16	4
14	14	44	6	27	15	0 ♑	29	18	5
14	18	37	7	28	15	1	23	19	6
14	22	31	8	29	16	2	18	20	8
14	26	25	9	♐	17	3	14	22	9
14	30	20	10	1	18	4	11	23	10
14	34	16	11	2	19	5	9	25	11
14	38	13	12	2	20	6	7	26	13
14	42	10	13	3	20	7	6	28	14
14	46	8	14	4	21	8	6	29	15
14	50	7	15	5	22	9	8	♓	17
14	54	7	16	6	23	10	11	2	18
14	58	7	17	7	24	11	15	4	19
15	2	8	18	8	25	12	20	6	21
15	6	9	19	9	26	13	27	8	22
15	10	12	20	9	27	14	35	9	23
15	14	15	21	10	27	15	43	11	24
15	18	19	22	11	28	16	52	13	26
15	22	23	23	12	29	18	3	14	27
15	26	29	24	13	♑	19	16	16	28
15	30	35	25	14	1	20	32	17	29
15	34	41	26	15	2	21	48	19	♉
15	38	49	27	16	3	23	8	21	2
15	42	57	28	17	4	24	29	22	3
15	47	6	29	18	5	25	51	24	5
15	51	15	30	18	6	27	15	26	6

Sidereal Time. H.	M.	S.	10 ♐ °	11 ♐ °	12 ♑ °	Ascen ♑ °	'	2 ♓ °	3 ♉ °
15	51	15	0	18	6	27	15	26	6
15	55	25	1	19	7	28	42	28	7
15	59	36	2	20	8	0 ♒	11	♈	9
16	3	48	3	21	9	1	42	1	10
16	8	0	4	22	10	3	16	3	11
16	12	13	5	23	11	4	53	5	12
16	16	26	6	24	12	6	32	7	14
16	20	40	7	25	13	8	13	9	15
16	24	55	8	26	14	9	57	11	16
16	29	10	9	27	16	11	44	12	17
16	33	26	10	28	17	13	34	14	18
16	37	42	11	29	18	15	26	16	20
16	41	59	12	♑	19	17	20	18	21
16	46	16	13	1	20	19	18	20	22
16	50	34	14	2	21	21	22	21	23
16	54	52	15	3	22	23	29	23	25
16	59	10	16	4	24	25	36	25	26
17	3	29	17	5	25	27	46	27	27
17	7	49	18	6	26	30	0	28	28
17	12	9	19	7	27	2 ♓	19	♉	29
17	16	29	20	8	29	4	40	2	♊
17	20	49	21	9	♒	7	2	3	1
17	25	9	22	10	1	9	26	5	2
17	29	30	23	11	3	11	54	7	3
17	33	51	24	12	4	14	24	8	5
17	38	12	25	13	5	17	0	10	6
17	42	34	26	14	7	19	33	11	7
17	46	55	27	15	8	22	6	13	8
17	51	17	28	16	10	24	40	14	9
17	55	38	29	17	11	27	23	16	10
18	0	0	30	18	13	30	0	17	11

Sidereal Time. H.	M.	S.	10 ♑ °	11 ♑ °	12 ♒ °	Ascen ♈ °	'	2 ♉ °	3 ♊ °
18	0	0	0	18	13	0	0	17	11
18	4	22	1	20	14	2	39	19	13
18	8	43	2	21	15	5	19	20	14
18	13	5	3	22	17	7	55	22	15
18	17	26	4	23	19	10	29	23	16
18	21	48	5	24	20	13	2	25	17
18	26	9	6	25	22	15	36	26	18
18	30	30	7	26	23	18	6	28	19
18	34	51	8	27	25	20	34	29	20
18	39	11	9	29	27	22	59	♊	21
18	43	31	10	♒	28	25	22	1	22
18	47	51	11	1	♓	27	42	2	23
18	52	11	12	2	2	29	58	4	24
18	56	31	13	3	3	2 ♉	13	5	25
19	0	50	14	4	5	4	24	6	26
19	5	8	15	6	7	6	30	8	27
19	9	26	16	7	9	8	36	9	28
19	13	44	17	8	10	10	40	10	29
19	18	1	18	9	12	12	39	11	♋
19	22	18	19	10	14	14	35	12	1
19	26	34	20	12	16	16	28	13	2
19	30	50	21	13	18	18	17	14	3
19	35	5	22	14	19	20	3	15	4
19	39	20	23	15	21	21	48	17	5
19	43	34	24	16	23	23	29	18	6
19	47	47	25	18	25	25	9	19	7
19	52	0	26	19	27	26	45	20	8
19	56	12	27	20	28	28	18	21	9
20	0	24	28	21	♈	29	49	22	10
20	4	35	29	22	2	1 ♊	19	23	11
20	8	45	30	24	4	2	45	24	12

Sidereal Time. H.	M.	S.	10 ♒ °	11 ♒ °	12 ♈ °	Ascen ♊ °	'	2 ♊ °	3 ♋ °
20	8	45	0	24	4	2	45	24	12
20	12	54	1	25	6	4	9	25	12
20	17	3	2	27	7	5	32	26	13
20	21	11	3	28	9	6	53	27	14
20	25	19	4	29	11	8	12	28	15
20	29	26	5	♓	13	9	27	29	16
20	33	31	6	2	14	10	43	♋	17
20	37	37	7	3	16	11	58	1	18
20	41	41	8	4	18	13	9	2	19
20	45	45	9	6	19	14	18	3	20
20	49	48	10	7	21	15	25	3	21
20	53	51	11	8	23	16	32	4	21
20	57	52	12	9	24	17	39	5	22
21	1	53	13	11	26	18	44	6	23
21	5	53	14	12	28	19	48	7	24
21	9	53	15	13	29	20	51	8	25
21	13	52	16	15	♉	21	53	9	26
21	17	50	17	16	2	22	53	10	27
21	21	47	18	17	4	23	52	10	28
21	25	44	19	19	5	24	51	11	28
21	29	40	20	20	7	25	48	12	29
21	33	35	21	22	8	26	44	13	♌
21	37	29	22	23	10	27	40	14	1
21	41	23	23	24	11	28	34	15	2
21	45	16	24	25	13	29	29	15	3
21	49	9	25	26	14	0 ♋	22	16	4
21	53	1	26	28	15	1	15	17	4
21	56	52	27	29	16	2	7	18	5
22	0	43	28	♈	18	2	57	19	6
22	4	33	29	2	19	3	48	19	7
22	8	23	30	3	20	4	38	20	8

Sidereal Time. H.	M.	S.	10 ♓ °	11 ♈ °	12 ♉ °	Ascen ♋ °	'	2 ♋ °	3 ♌ °
22	8	23	0	3	20	4	38	20	8
22	12	12	1	4	21	5	28	21	8
22	16	0	2	6	23	6	17	22	9
22	19	48	3	7	24	7	5	22	10
22	23	35	4	8	25	7	53	23	11
22	27	22	5	9	26	8	42	24	12
22	31	8	6	10	28	9	29	25	13
22	34	54	7	12	29	10	16	26	14
22	38	40	8	13	♊	11	2	26	14
22	42	25	9	14	1	11	47	27	15
22	46	9	10	15	2	12	31	28	16
22	49	53	11	17	3	13	16	29	17
22	53	37	12	18	4	14	1	29	18
22	57	20	13	19	5	14	45	♌	19
23	1	3	14	20	6	15	28	1	19
23	4	46	15	21	7	16	11	2	20
23	8	28	16	22	8	16	54	2	21
23	12	10	17	24	9	17	37	3	22
23	15	52	18	25	10	18	20	4	23
23	19	34	19	26	11	19	3	5	24
23	23	15	20	27	12	19	45	5	24
23	26	56	21	29	13	20	26	6	25
23	30	37	22	♉	14	21	8	7	26
23	34	18	23	1	15	21	50	7	27
23	37	58	24	2	16	22	31	8	28
23	41	39	25	3	17	23	12	9	28
23	45	19	26	4	18	23	53	9	29
23	49	0	27	5	19	24	33	10	♍
23	52	40	28	6	20	25	15	11	1
23	56	20	29	8	21	25	56	12	2
24	0	0	30	9	22	26	36	12	3

Sidereal Time.			10 ♈	11 ♉	12 ♊	Ascen ♋		2 ♌	3 ♍
H.	M.	S.	°	°	°	°	′	°	°
0	0	0	0	9	22	26	36	12	3
0	3	40	1	10	23	27	17	13	3
0	7	20	2	11	24	27	56	14	4
0	11	0	3	12	25	28	42	15	5
0	14	41	4	13	25	29	17	15	6
0	18	21	5	14	26	29	55	16	7
0	22	2	6	15	27	0♌	34	17	8
0	25	42	7	16	28	1	14	18	8
0	29	23	8	17	29	1	55	18	9
0	33	4	9	18	♋	2	33	19	10
0	36	45	10	19	1	3	14	20	11
0	40	26	11	20	1	3	54	20	12
0	44	8	12	21	2	4	33	21	13
0	47	50	13	22	3	5	12	22	14
0	51	32	14	23	4	5	52	23	15
0	55	14	15	24	5	6	30	23	15
0	58	57	16	25	6	7	9	24	16
1	2	40	17	26	6	7	50	25	17
1	6	23	18	27	7	8	30	26	18
1	10	7	19	28	8	9	9	26	19
1	13	51	20	29	9	9	48	27	19
1	17	35	21	♊	10	10	28	28	20
1	21	20	22	1	10	11	8	28	21
1	25	6	23	2	11	11	48	29	22
1	28	52	24	3	12	12	28	♍	23
1	32	38	25	4	13	13	8	1	24
1	36	25	26	5	14	13	48	1	25
1	40	12	27	6	14	14	28	2	25
1	44	0	28	7	15	15	8	3	26
1	47	48	29	8	16	15	48	4	27
1	51	37	30	9	17	16	28	4	28

Sidereal Time.			10 ♉	11 ♊	12 ♋	Ascen ♌		2 ♍	3 ♍
H.	M.	S.	°	°	°	°	′	°	°
1	51	37	0	9	17	16	28	4	28
1	55	27	1	10	18	17	8	5	29
1	59	17	2	11	19	17	48	6	♎
2	3	8	3	12	19	18	28	7	1
2	6	59	4	13	20	19	9	8	2
2	10	51	5	14	21	19	49	9	2
2	14	44	6	15	22	20	29	9	3
2	18	37	7	16	22	21	10	10	4
2	22	31	8	17	23	21	51	11	5
2	26	25	9	18	24	22	32	11	6
2	30	20	10	19	25	23	14	12	7
2	34	16	11	20	25	23	55	13	8
2	38	13	12	21	26	24	36	14	9
2	42	10	13	22	27	25	17	15	10
2	46	8	14	23	28	25	58	15	11
2	50	7	15	24	29	26	40	16	12
2	54	7	16	25	29	27	22	17	12
2	58	7	17	26	♌	28	4	18	13
3	2	8	18	27	1	28	46	18	14
3	6	9	19	27	2	29	28	19	15
3	10	12	20	28	3	0♍	12	20	16
3	14	15	21	29	3	0	54	21	17
3	18	19	22	♋	4	1	36	22	18
3	22	23	23	1	5	2	20	22	19
3	26	29	24	2	6	3	2	23	20
3	30	35	25	3	7	3	45	24	21
3	34	41	26	4	7	4	28	25	22
3	38	49	27	5	8	5	11	26	23
3	42	57	28	6	9	5	54	27	24
3	47	6	29	7	10	6	38	27	25
3	51	15	30	8	11	7	21	28	25

Sidereal Time.			10 ♊	11 ♋	12 ♌	Ascen ♍		2 ♍	3 ♎
H.	M.	S.	°	°	°	°	′	°	°
3	51	15	0	8	11	7	21	28	25
3	55	25	1	9	12	8	5	29	26
3	59	36	2	10	12	8	49	♎	27
4	3	48	3	10	13	9	33	1	28
4	8	0	4	11	14	10	17	2	29
4	12	13	5	12	15	11	2	2	♏
4	16	26	6	13	16	11	46	3	1
4	20	40	7	14	17	12	30	4	2
4	24	55	8	15	17	13	15	5	3
4	29	10	9	16	18	14	0	6	4
4	33	26	10	17	19	14	45	7	5
4	37	42	11	18	20	15	30	8	6
4	41	59	12	19	21	16	15	8	7
4	46	16	13	20	21	17	0	9	8
4	50	34	14	21	22	17	45	10	9
4	54	52	15	22	23	18	30	11	10
4	59	10	16	23	24	19	16	12	11
5	3	29	17	24	25	20	3	13	12
5	7	49	18	25	26	20	49	14	13
5	12	9	19	26	27	21	35	14	14
5	16	29	20	26	28	22	20	15	14
5	20	49	21	27	28	23	6	16	15
5	25	9	22	28	29	23	51	17	16
5	29	30	23	29	♍	24	37	18	17
5	33	51	24	♌	1	25	23	19	18
5	38	12	25	1	2	26	9	20	19
5	42	34	26	2	3	26	55	21	20
5	46	55	27	3	4	27	41	21	21
5	51	17	28	4	4	28	27	22	22
5	55	38	29	5	5	29	13	23	23
6	0	0	30	6	6	30	0	24	24

Sidereal Time.			10 ♋	11 ♌	12 ♍	Ascen ♎		2 ♎	3 ♏
H.	M.	S.	°	°	°	°	′	°	°
6	0	0	0	6	6	0	0	24	24
6	4	22	1	7	7	0	47	25	25
6	8	43	2	8	8	1	33	26	26
6	13	5	3	9	9	2	19	27	27
6	17	26	4	10	10	3	5	27	28
6	21	48	5	11	10	3	51	28	29
6	26	9	6	12	11	4	37	29	♐
6	30	30	7	13	12	5	23	♏	1
6	34	51	8	14	13	6	9	1	2
6	39	11	9	15	14	6	55	2	3
6	43	31	10	16	15	7	40	2	4
6	47	51	11	16	16	8	26	3	4
6	52	11	12	17	16	9	12	4	5
6	56	31	13	18	17	9	58	5	6
7	0	50	14	19	18	10	43	6	7
7	5	8	15	20	19	11	28	7	8
7	9	26	16	21	20	12	14	8	9
7	13	44	17	22	21	12	59	8	10
7	18	1	18	23	22	13	45	9	11
7	22	18	19	24	23	14	30	10	12
7	26	34	20	25	24	15	15	11	13
7	30	50	21	26	25	16	0	12	14
7	35	5	22	27	25	16	45	13	15
7	39	20	23	28	26	17	30	13	16
7	43	34	24	29	27	18	15	14	17
7	47	47	25	♍	28	18	59	15	18
7	52	0	26	1	29	19	43	16	19
7	56	12	27	2	29	20	27	17	20
8	0	24	28	3	♎	21	11	18	20
8	4	35	29	4	1	21	56	18	21
8	8	45	30	5	2	22	40	19	22

Sidereal Time.			10 ♌	11 ♍	12 ♎	Ascen ♎		2 ♏	3 ♐
H.	M.	S.	°	°	°	°	′	°	°
8	8	45	0	5	2	22	40	19	22
8	12	54	1	5	3	23	24	20	23
8	17	3	2	6	3	24	7	21	24
8	21	11	3	7	4	24	50	22	25
8	25	19	4	8	5	25	34	23	26
8	29	26	5	9	6	26	18	23	27
8	33	31	6	10	7	27	1	24	28
8	37	37	7	11	8	27	44	25	29
8	41	41	8	12	8	28	26	26	♑
8	45	45	9	13	9	29	8	27	1
8	49	48	10	14	10	29	50	27	2
8	53	51	11	15	11	0♏	32	28	3
8	57	52	12	16	12	1	15	29	4
9	1	53	13	17	12	1	58	♐	4
9	5	53	14	18	13	2	39	1	5
9	9	53	15	18	14	3	21	1	6
9	13	52	16	19	15	4	3	2	7
9	17	50	17	20	16	4	44	3	8
9	21	47	18	21	16	5	26	3	9
9	25	44	19	22	17	6	7	4	10
9	29	40	20	23	18	6	48	5	11
9	33	35	21	24	18	7	29	5	12
9	37	29	22	25	19	8	9	6	13
9	41	23	23	26	20	8	50	7	14
9	45	16	24	27	21	9	31	8	15
9	49	9	25	28	22	10	11	9	16
9	53	1	26	28	23	10	51	9	17
9	56	52	27	29	23	11	32	10	18
10	0	43	28	♎	24	12	12	11	19
10	4	33	29	1	25	12	53	12	20
10	8	23	30	2	26	13	33	13	20

Sidereal Time.			10 ♍	11 ♎	12 ♎	Ascen ♏		2 ♐	3 ♑
H.	M.	S.	°	°	°	°	′	°	°
10	8	23	0	2	26	13	33	13	20
10	12	12	1	3	26	14	13	14	21
10	16	0	2	4	27	14	53	15	22
10	19	48	3	5	28	15	33	15	23
10	23	35	4	5	29	16	13	16	24
10	27	22	5	6	29	16	52	17	25
10	31	8	6	7	♏	17	32	18	26
10	34	54	7	8	1	18	12	19	27
10	38	40	8	9	2	18	52	20	28
10	42	25	9	10	2	19	31	20	29
10	46	9	10	11	3	20	11	21	♒
10	49	53	11	11	4	20	50	22	1
10	53	37	12	12	4	21	30	23	2
10	57	20	13	13	5	22	9	24	3
11	1	3	14	14	6	22	49	24	4
11	4	46	15	15	7	23	28	25	5
11	8	28	16	16	7	24	8	26	6
11	12	10	17	17	8	24	47	27	8
11	15	52	18	17	9	25	27	28	9
11	19	34	19	18	10	26	6	29	10
11	23	15	20	19	10	26	45	♑	11
11	26	56	21	20	11	27	25	0	12
11	30	37	22	21	12	28	5	1	13
11	34	18	23	22	13	28	44	2	14
11	37	58	24	23	13	29	24	3	15
11	41	39	25	23	14	0♐	4	4	16
11	45	19	26	24	15	0	43	5	17
11	49	0	27	25	15	1	23	6	18
11	52	40	28	26	16	2	3	6	19
11	56	20	29	27	17	2	43	7	20
12	0	0	30	27	17	3	23	8	20

Astrology

15 to turn it into degrees and minutes of the Equator, you will obtain 55° 30′, which are the number of degrees which pass over the Midheaven from birth until sunset. At the rate of 1 degree for every year of life, this corresponds to 55½ years of age, when the subject of this horoscope would come under the adverse influence of the Sun opposition Ascendant, and would suffer some serious ill health of a feverish nature, incident to the throat (the part ruled by Taurus, the sign in which the Sun is situate). This is how predictions are made, but of this more anon.

If I wished to know what particular part of the Zodiac one is subject to in any particular year of life—that is to say, what part of the Zodiac is rising—I add 1 degree for every year to the Midheaven at birth and thus obtain a new Midheaven, under which, in the Tables of Houses, I find the Ascendant which rules the year. Thus in the case of one born on the 1st of May at 3.30 p.m. the 30th year comes under the Midheaven of Leo 2, which is 30 degrees further advanced than Cancer 2, and under Leo 2 in the 10th House I find the Ascendant to be in Libra 24.7, which is the Ascendant governing that year of life. The meaning and importance of these calculations will appear at a later stage of this exposition.

When a degree is on the Midheaven or the 10th House it is said to "culminate," and when on the horizon Eastward it is said to "ascend."

The Midheaven is often called the "M.C." (Medium Coeli), and the opposite point is called the "I.C." (Imaum Coeli). They are the points of the Ecliptic which cut through the meridian of a place at any given time.

CHAPTER IV

PLANETARY TRANSITS

IN order that prognostications made from the horoscope of birth may be pointed as to time it is necessary to know the positions of the planets for several years in advance. Such calculations are easily effected by a knowledge of the periods of the planets—that is to say, the times in which they return to the same positions about the same time of the year. Thus Uranus returns to its place after a period of 84 years, Saturn does so after 59 years, Jupiter in 83 years, Mars in 79 years, in all cases almost to the day. Mercury also returns in 79 years. But as very few people possess records of the planets' places for these long periods, the following table of the longitudes of the planets for the next 12 years has been prepared. The positions are given for the 1st of each month, and the longitudes held by the planets are given in even degrees.

These tables are very useful in tracing the transits that occur in connection with the horoscope for the year. Thus we have found that by adding the number of degrees corresponding to the age of a person to the Midheaven at birth, we obtain the Progressed Midheaven,

Astrology

Month	1905 ♆	♅	♄	♃	♂	1908 ♆	♅	♄	♃	♂
January	♋6	♑0	♒19	♈21	♎24	♋13	♑13	♓22	♌12	♓24
February	5	2	22	24	♏10	12	14	25	8	♈15
March	4	3	26	29	20	11	16	28	5	♉5
April	5	4	29	♉5	26	12	17	♈2	4	26
May	6	4	♓1	12	19	13	17	5	5	♊16
June	7	3	3	20	10	14	16	8	9	♋7
July	8	2	2	26	11	15	15	10	14	28
August	9	0	1	♊2	21	16	14	10	21	♌16
September	9	0	♒29	6	♐6	16	13	8	28	♍5
October	10	0	27	6	25	17	13	6	♍4	24
November	10	1	26	4	♑17	17	13	4	9	♎14
December	9	3	27	0	♒11	16	14	3	13	♏4

Month	1906 ♆	♅	♄	♃	♂	1909 ♆	♅	♄	♃	♂
January	♋9	♑5	♒29	♉27	♓4	♋15	♑16	♈4	♍14	♏24
February	8	6	♓3	27	27	14	18	6	13	♐15
March	7	8	6	29	♈18	13	20	9	9	♑4
April	8	8	10	♊4	♉11	14	21	13	6	24
May	9	8	13	10	♊2	15	21	17	4	♒14
June	10	7	14	17	23	16	20	20	6	♓4
July	11	6	15	24	♋13	17	19	22	9	23
August	12	5	14	♋0	♌3	18	18	23	15	♈4
September	12	4	12	5	23	18	17	22	21	8
October	13	4	9	10	♍12	19	17	20	28	♓26
November	13	5	8	11	♎1	19	17	18	♎4	25
December	12	7	8	9	20	18	19	16	9	♈4

Month	1907 ♆	♅	♄	♃	♂	1910 ♆	♅	♄	♃	♂
January	♋11	♑9	♓9	♋5	♏11	♋17	♑20	♈16	♎13	♈18
February	10	10	14	2	29	16	22	18	14	♉5
March	9	12	17	1	♐15	15	24	21	13	22
April	10	12	21	3	♑2	16	25	24	9	♊11
May	11	12	24	7	13	17	25	28	6	♋0
June	12	12	26	13	18	18	25	♉1	4	19
July	13	11	27	19	13	19	24	4	6	♌8
August	14	9	27	26	6	20	22	6	9	♍17
September	14	8	25	♌3	11	20	21	6	15	♍17
October	15	8	23	8	24	21	21	4	21	♎6
November	15	9	21	♒13	13	21	22	2	28	27
December	14	11	21	14	♓2	20	23	0	♏4	♏17

44

Planetary Transits

Month.	1911. ♆	♅	♄	♃	♂	1914. ♆	♅	♄	♃	♂
January	♋20	♑24	♈29	♏9	♐8	♋26	♒7	♊12	♑26	♋16
February	20	26	♉0	13	♑1	25	8	11	♒3	7
March	19	28	2	14	29	24	9	11	9	8
April	20	29	6	13	♒14	25	11	13	15	17
May	20	29	10	9	♓7	26	11	16	20	♌1
June	21	29	14	6	♈0	27	11	20	22	17
July	22	28	17	5	21	28	10	24	22	♍3
August	23	27	19	6	♉12	29	9	28	19	22
September	23	26	20	10	29	♌0	8	♋0	15	♎13
October	24	25	19	15	♊9	0	7	2	13	♏1
November	24	25	17	22	9	0	7	2	13	29
December	23	27	14	28	♉28	♋29	8	0	17	♐15

Month.	1912. ♆	♅	♄	♃	♂	1915. ♆	♅	♄	♃	♂
January	♋22	♑28	♉13	♐5	♉24	♋28	♒10	♊27	♒28	♑8
February	21	♒0	13	10	♊1	28	12	26	29	♒2
March	20	1	15	14	12	27	13	25	♓6	25
April	21	3	18	15	29	28	15	26	14	♓16
May	22	3	23	14	♋14	28	15	29	20	♈12
June	23	3	26	10	♌2	29	14	♋3	26	♉6
July	24	2	29	7	20	♌0	13	6	28	27
August	25	1	♊2	5	♍10	1	12	10	28	♊19
September	25	0	4	7	29	1	11	13	26	♋9
Octooer	26	♑29	3	10	♎19	2	11	15	22	27
November	26	29	2	16	♏10	2	12	16	19	♌14
December	25	♒0	♉20	23	♐1	1	12	15	19	25

Month.	1913. ♆	♅	♄	♃	♂	1916. ♆	♅	♄	♃	♂
Jaunary	♋24	♒3	♉27	♑0	♐28	♌1	♒14	♋13	♓23	♍1
February	24	4	27	6	♑17	0	15	10	28	♌23
March	23	5	28	12	♒8	♋29	17	9	♈4	13
April	24	7	♊0	16	♓2	♌0	18	10	12	13
May	24	7	4	18	25	1	19	11	19	20
June	25	7	8	17	♈18	2	19	15	26	♍2
July	26	6	12	13	♉10	3	19	19	♉1	17
August	27	5	15	10	♊2	4	18	23	5	♎6
September	27	4	17	8	21	4	17	26	6	25
October	28	3	18	9	♋9	5	16	29	3	♏16
November	28	3	17	13	21	5	16	♌0	♈29	♐8
December	27	4	15	18	24	4	16	0	26	♑0

Astrology

and in the Tables of Houses we may also find the corresponding Progressed Ascendant. By adding the same number of degrees to the place of the Sun at birth we obtain also the Progressed position of the Sun.

Now a transit of one of the major planets over any of these points, namely, the Midheaven or Ascendant at birth, the Sun or Moon at birth, the Midheaven, Ascendant, and Sun in the progress, will produce marked effects on the fortunes and health of the Subject, corresponding to the nature of the planet which makes the transit.

Thus we have seen that the Midheaven at the birth on the 1st of May, 1890, at 3.30 p.m., was Cancer 2 degrees, and the Ascendant Libra 2. Referring to the Tables, we find that in 1905 Saturn will form the opposition of the Midheaven in Capricornus 2 in February, July, and November, so that these will be periods of reversal, sudden and unexpected complications and changes. Also the Sun at birth being in Taurus 11 receives the transit of Jupiter in April, 1905, so that this month will be productive of some amelioration of evils, or direct benefits.

When two or more planets concur in a transit of any of the Significators the results are so much the more forcible and effective.

CHAPTER V

TABLE OF ECLIPSES

THE following Table of the Eclipses that take place during the twelve years will be found of considerable use in forecasting the effects which will follow, not only on the individual, but also on nations and countries. Thus should any of the Eclipses fall on the place of a Significator in a horoscope, it will have the most sinister effect upon the life and fortunes. Certain countries are ruled by certain signs, a matter which has been determined from observation ever since the days of Claudius Ptolemy A. D. 130, and Eclipses falling therein have the effect of disturbing the government of those countries, producing effects of the worst kind. (See Sect. IV., chap. 6).

TABLE OF ECLIPSES, 1905-1916.

1905.—18th February, Moon eclipsed in Leo 29.
    5th March, Sun eclipsed in Pisces 14.
    14th August, Moon eclipsed in Aquarius 21.
    30th August, Sun eclipsed in Virgo 6.

1906.—8th February, Moon eclipsed in Leo 19.
    22nd February, Sun eclipsed in Pisces 3.

Astrology

    20th July, Sun eclipsed in Cancer 27.
    3rd August, Moon eclipsed in Aquarius 10.
    18th August, Sun eclipsed in Leo 24.
    14th January, Sun eclipsed in Capricornus 23

1907.—28th January, Moon eclipsed in Aquarius 7.
    9th July, Sun eclipsed in Cancer 16.
    23rd July, Moon eclipsed in Leo 4.

1908.—3rd January, Sun eclipsed in Capricornus 12.
    28th August, Sun eclipsed in Virgo 4.
    7th December, Moon eclipsed in Gemini 14.
    22nd December, Sun eclipsed in Sagittarius 30.

1909.—3rd June, Moon eclipsed in Sagittarius 12.
    17th June, Sun eclipsed in Gemini 25.
    26th November, Moon eclipsed in Gemini 3.
    12th December, Sun eclipsed in Sagittarius 19.

1910.—9th May, Sun eclipsed in Taurus 18.
    22nd May, Moon eclipsed in Sagittarius 0.
    1st November, Sun eclipsed in Scorpio 7.
    15th November, Moon eclipsed in Taurus 21.

1911.—28th April, Sun eclipsed in Taurus 7.
    20th October, Sun eclipsed in Libra 26.

1912.—1st April, Moon eclipsed in Libra 11.
    16th April, Sun eclipsed in Aries 25.
    25th September, Moon eclipsed in Aries 1.
    10th October, Sun eclipsed in Libra 16.

Table of Eclipses

1913.—21st March, Moon eclipsed in Virgo 30.
   5th April, Sun eclipsed in Aries 15.
   30th August, Sun eclipsed in Virgo 7.
   14th September, Moon eclipsed in Virgo 20.
   28th September, Sun eclipsed in Libra 4.

1914.—24th February, Sun eclipsed in Pisces 5.
   9th March, Moon eclipsed in Virgo 18.
   21st August, Moon eclipsed in Aquarius 27.
   3rd September, Sun eclipsed in Virgo 10.

1915.—13th February, Sun eclipsed in Aquarius 24.
   9th August, Sun eclipsed in Leo 16.

1916.—18th January, Moon eclipsed in Cancer 27.
   3rd February, Sun eclipsed in Aquarius 13.
   14th July, Moon eclipsed in Capricornus 21.
   29th July, Sun eclipsed in Leo 5.

In illustration of the effects of Eclipses in the horoscope of birth, we may refer to the horoscope of His Majesty King Edward VII., wherein we find the sun situated in the 17th degree of the sign Scorpio, which rules the excretory system. In May, 1902, there was an Eclipse of the Sun in opposition to this position, and within five weeks of the Eclipse the King was struck down with appendicitis on the eve of the Coronation Ceremony. This was foretold in many of the journals devoted to the exposition of Astrology, and in Moore's Almanac for the month of June, 1902, the hieroglyphic clearly pointed to the danger that beset the august Sovereign. Indeed, I was able to say with perfect assurance that the Corona-

Astrology

tion would not take place on the date appointed, and gave the exact date at which the King would be struck down with what I conceived to be a mortal illness. But fortunately at that time the Moon was conjoined to Jupiter in the progress and this saved the life. The Moon was then setting in the horoscope of birth, according to the measure of time already given, namely, one degree of Right Ascension for one year of life, and Saturn was on the Midheaven.

The Eclipse of June 6, 1853, was in the Midheaven at Cumana on the Spanish Main and in five weeks there followed a terrible earthquake which killed 4,000 people and destroyed all the property. In May, 1901, there was an Eclipse on the 8th of May which fell in the meridian of St. Pierre, Martinique, and the same day there was a fearful devastation of the place by the eruption of Mont Pelèe.

Instances might be multiplied to show that the effects of Eclipses are of the most striking and effective nature.

SECTION III

HOW TO READ THE HOROSCOPE

CHAPTER I

THE PLANETS IN THE HOUSES

It is impossible to categorically state the effects which are due to the positions of the planets in the several Houses, because very much depends upon the signs they are in and the aspects they have from other planets.

The means of judging the effects is very simple, when once the natures of the planets and the dominion of the several Houses have been thoroughly digested. Thus, it is first necessary to see in what House a planet is situated. Then consider the nature of the planet in the following concrete manner:

Neptune means chaos, confusion, deception.
Uranus, eccentricity, originality, estrangement.
Saturn, privation, hindrance, denial.
Jupiter, affluence, fruitfulness, increase.
Sun, dignities, honors.
Mars, excess, impulse, quarrels.
Venus, peace, happiness, agreement.

Astrology

Mercury, commerce, versatility, adaptability.

Moon, changes, publicity.

Now look to the things that are governed by the House in which any particular planet is situated at the moment of birth (Sect. I., chap. iii.).

Suppose Saturn to be found in the 11th House. Saturn is "privation" and the 11th House is the domain of "Friends." Hence a paucity of friends, or such as there may be are evil or unfortunate to the subject. Jupiter in the 2nd House, in the same manner, would signify "increase" of "money and possessions." Mars in the 7th would indicate "quarrels" with "partners"; and so on. Each planet reflects its own nature upon the affairs governed by the House in which it is found at the moment of birth.

It will not infrequently happen, however, that there are more than one planet in the same House. Suppose two planets to occupy the same House. In such case one may be good (Jupiter), and the other evil (Mars). It is then necessary to take first that which first comes to the horizon or Midheaven, that is to say, the one which is in the earlier part of the House, and next that which follows. Thus Saturn followed by Jupiter in the 11th House, would signify misfortune by means of advisers and friends, followed at a later period in the life by some great good through the same source. The degrees which separate the planets will indicate the years which elapse between these changes of fortune. Similarly if there be more than two planets in the same House; in such cases you may safely predict many changes in that department of life which the House is said to rule.

The Planets in the Houses

But the fact of a planet being in a House is not of itself sufficient evidence from which to make a judgment. The aspects which that planet has must also be considered, for in this matter Saturn when throwing a good aspect to any of the Significators—the Sun, Moon, Ascendant or Midheaven, and well aspected by other planets, is to be preferred to Jupiter when the latter is badly placed and aspected; for Jupiter has his own ill effects, and Saturn has his good influences. Jupiter is only a benefic when acting by conjunction or good aspect with another planet, and Saturn is only a malefic when acting by conjunction or evil aspect.

These things being duly considered, it is possible to arrive, with even brief experience, at the results that are signified by the planets in the several Houses.

CHAPTER II

THE CONSTITUTION

THE Sun is the chief significator of the constitution, and the aspects he holds to the other planets are to be considered. Thus if he be found in good aspect, or at least not in evil aspect, to the other planets, the constitution may be judged as sound.

When, however, the Sun is afflicted by some planets and assisted by others, there will be only a moderate constitution, and judgment has to be made as to which influence predominates, the good or evil. When the afflicting planets are angular—that is to say, in the 1st, 4th, 7th, or 10th Houses—the congenital or hereditary tendency to organic disease is by that circumstance so much the stronger. But when the assisting planets are angular, the predisposition to disease is considerably mitigated, and in most cases entirely overcome.

The predisposition of the body to affections of a constitutional nature is to be judged from the prevalence of evil aspects to the Sun, and the parts of the body liable to be affected are judged from the Signs which are occupied by the afflicting bodies.

The various affections due to the several planets have already been cited (Sect. I., chap. i.). The Signs are grouped for purposes of pathological study as follows:—

The Constitution

The Movable Signs—Aries, Cancer, Libra, and Capricornus—have relation to the head, stomach, skin, kidneys, liver, and spine.

The Fixed Signs—Taurus, Leo, Scorpio, and Aquarius—are related to the throat, heart, blood, and excretory system.

The Common Signs—Gemini, Virgo, Sagittarius, and Pisces—are related to the lungs, bowels, and nervous system.

It will also be advisable to read Sect. I., chap. ii., in order to determine the special points liable to affections, the nature of the affection being judged solely by the planet which casts the malefic aspect to the Sun.

When the Sun is found to be afflicted by several planets, and at the same time there is no assistance from the good aspects or conjunctions of other bodies, then the constitution is deemed faulty and liable to early disruption. But when there are several planets afflicting and at the same time some benefic influences from others, it is probable that there will be prolonged disease and physical weakness, though life will continue.

Death in infancy occurs when the malefic planets are immediately rising or culminating at the birth in evil aspect to the luminary which at the time may be above the horizon. Also when there are malefic planets immediately setting or passing the nadir, in evil aspect to the luminary below the horizon. But when there are mitigating influences from the good aspects of the benefic planets, or the luminaries, the malefic planets will not induce death, but there will be great difficulty in rearing.

CHAPTER III

HEALTH AND SICKNESS

The aspects of the Moon are the chief consideration in the matter of sickness. If the Moon be found to be afflicted by the evil aspects of several planets, and no assistance be given by the good aspects of others, then the health will be precarious and frequent spells of illness will result. The Moon being well aspected and not in any way afflicted, shows that the health will be well established, and that there will be immunity from sickness of all sorts.

The considerations necessary to be made in this matter are similar to those which have been cited in regard to the Sun and the constitution, except that we substitute the Moon for the Sun. For, whereas the Sun governs the vital power in man, the Moon governs the functional powers, and whereas the Sun denotes those affections which are congenital or hereditary, the Moon denotes such as are brought about by causes after birth. Similarly, the Sun denotes affections which are incidental to the body, while the Moon denotes such as are accidental thereto.

Health and Sickness

These points being borne in mind, they may be memorised at sight:—

Sun.	Moon.
Organic.	Functional.
Hereditary.	Acquired.
Incidental.	Accidental.

But it should be observed that the constitution may be strong and the health may be at the same time very bad, or, on the other hand, the health may be good and the constitution may be weak. In the first case, there would be a long life of considerable suffering from ill-health; and in the second case, there would be little or no ill-health for some considerable time, but the constitution would give way and the vital powers become depleted by the first serious illness that occurred.

Only when the Sun and Moon are both unafflicted by evil aspects or conjunctions, the health and constitution are both good, and there is every indication of a robust and vigorous life reaching to a ripe old age.

When the Sun and Moon are both heavily afflicted, and there is no assistance given by good aspects, there is every probability of death in infancy, or before reaching maturity.

For reasons which are allied to the connection existing between the constitution and the health, the good aspect of the Moon to the Sun at birth is an excellent augury, for it indicates co-ordination between the organic and functional. Where this co-ordination exists there is always considerable power of recuperation, so that illness is easily overcome and the balance of power restored in the system.

Astrology

Malefic planets rising and afflicting either the Sun or Moon indicate prolonged ill-health, and most frequently some permanent hurt to the body.

When predisposition to illness is shown in the horoscope, the particular affection can be determined by the Sign which the afflicting planets hold. Thus if Saturn afflict the Moon from Aries, you will judge some hurts and obstructions in the head, chills and colds, influenza, coryza, &c. Similarly Mars in Leo would indicate functional defects of the heart due to accelerated action and overstrain, such as result from fevers.

A good aspect of the planets Jupiter and Venus is of material help in counteracting the influence of malefic aspects or evil positions.

Thus it will be seen that the health may be judged entirely apart from the constitution, the planets which are in aspect to the Moon being of first consideration, and next those which may be rising at the time of birth.

CHAPTER VI

HOW TO READ CHARACTER AND DISPOSITION

PTOLEMY says: "Mercury is the ruler of the rational soul, the Moon of the animal soul." By this he would mean, no doubt, that Mercury has relation to the faculty of the mind, while the Moon is related to brain function. There are certain attributes of the mind which are distinctive of the human being, and certain other qualities which are common to man and the lower animals. These latter are under the dominion of the Moon, while Mercury has chief signification of the rational faculties.

The position and aspects of the Moon and Mercury are therefore to be considered in making judgment of the mental endowments and disposition of the subject.

Planets that are in conjunction or aspect to either the Moon or Mercury will impress their nature strongly on the character and disposition. The natures of the planets have already been recited (Sect. I., chap. i.), and it is therefore only necessary to consider further, in this connection, the nature of the aspect that is thrown to the Mental Significators by the other bodies. Thus the Sun being in trine to the Moon will give a proper degree

Astrology

of independence and dignity, while the square aspect or opposition of the Sun would indicate an excess of pride, harmful to the subject in his ordinary relationships. In the same manner, the good aspect of Jupiter would show benevolence and regulated philanthropy, while the opposition or other evil aspect of the same body would indicate extravagance and ostentatious display of charity.

The good and bad aspects of the planets may be summed up in a few lines as follows:—

In Good Aspect.	In Evil Aspect.
Neptune—Genius, inspiration.	Insanity, obsession.
Uranus—Originality, invention.	Obstinacy, eccentricity.
Saturn—Steadfastness, fidelity.	Deceitfulness, suspicion.
Jupiter—Benevolence, joviality.	Ostentation, profligacy.
Mars—Energy, executiveness.	Impulse, destructiveness.
Sun—Dignity, independence.	Vanity, egotism.
Venus—Affability, art.	Self-indulgence, disorderliness.
Mercury—Alertness, ingenuity.	Inquisitiveness, meddling.
Moon—Grace, idealism.	Inconstancy, awkwardness.

The general trend of the disposition and habit of mind is judged by the position of the majority of the planets, according to the "Constitution" of the Signs they occupy. Thus, the majority of the planets being in—

Cardinal or Movable Signs indicates executive ability, business aptitude, pioneer spirit, ambition, capability to cut out a line in life for oneself, and to make headway against difficulties. Such persons are usually the foremost in their particular sphere of life, and are always found in the most progressive movements, reforms, &c.

Fixed Signs—Stability, patience, endurance, method, caution, and diplomacy. Such persons are apt to become the originators of schools of thought, policies,

How to Read Character

and schemes. They have fixity of purpose, determination, independence, and pivotal stability. They sit still and the world revolves around them.

Flexed or Common Signs—Versatility, flexibility, suavity, adaptability, and lack of originality. Such people usually have too many irons in the fire, and take in hand more than they can bring to satisfactory conclusion. This is due to their versatility. They have a superficial knowledge of many things, but lack the persistence to bring that knowledge to practical effect. At the same time their adaptability is the occasion of many successes in life, and their agreeableness, sympathy, and suavity create many friends for them.

In the Wheel of Life the cardinal signs denote the rim or tyre which is ever on the move, having the greatest acceleration. The Common Signs represent the spokes of the wheel, uniting the tyre to the nave, and in that sense representing the power of adaptability. The Fixed Signs represent the nave, which remains quiescent and still, being useful by that pivotal stability and apparent non-entity.

Thus, while the Sign-groupings of the planets are useful in giving the keynote of the nature and disposition, the particular faculties and characteristics are to be judged only from the aspects of the planets to the Moon and Mercury. Further, it will be noted that those planets which occupy the 3rd and 9th Houses, and those also which are just rising at the moment of birth, will strongly impress themselves on the nature, apart from any aspects they may hold to the Mental Rulers. This is on account of the natural relationship of those Houses to the mind and its means of expression.

Astrology

Due attention must be paid to the position and aspects of those planets which are in aspect to the Mental Rulers, for if they be badly placed, in uncongenial signs, and themselves badly aspected by other planets, they will not act with the same directness and force as they otherwise would do.

It is of course admitted, in all astrological inquiries, that the effects of heredity, training, and association count for something. A man who is generated from a vitiated parentage, badly nourished and imperfectly trained, cannot be expected, even with the best aspects, to manifest the highest faculties in their fullest or most perfect expressions. I have not the slightest doubt that many a clodpole was born under similar aspects to those which obtained at the birth of Shakspere, Raphael, Newton, or Cæsar. I am not dismayed. *Non gli astri muovono solamente per Roma!* Who shall tell the tale of the world's starved, neglected, and submerged genius? We are doing the right thing, at all events, in keeping the school-door wide open.

But to continue. The inspirational and ardent temperament is indicated by the majority of planets being in Fiery signs. The mental or intellectual temperament is shown by the majority in Aerial signs. The psychic or emotional temperament by the majority in Watery signs, and the practical or sordid temperament by the majority being in Earthy signs.

The rising sign at birth often impresses itself strongly on the mind of the Subject, and its characteristics are those which belong to the planet which governs it, and the "elemental" nature of the sign itself.

Thus you have the chief keys to the estimate of char-

How to Read Character

acter in the individual, and when once the student is convinced by experience of the paramount reliability of this method of character-delineation, its uses will need no special pointing.

Mental and Brain Disorders

When either the Moon or Mercury is afflicted by the malefic planets, that is to say, when Neptune, Uranus, Saturn, or Mars are in conjunction or evil aspect with the mental Significators, and there be no relieving aspect from the benefic planets, Jupiter, Venus, or the Sun, then there is every predisposition to affections of the brain and nervous system. This is the more to be feared when the Moon or Mercury is afflicted in the flexed or common signs. This observation has been scientifically established by Mr. A. G. Trent, in his little work entitled "The Soul and the Stars," to which the student is referred for a mass of statistical evidence.

CHAPTER V

FINANCIAL PROSPECTS

Look to the planets which are in the 2nd House, and the aspects to them. If any planet be therein, and well aspected by others, the financial condition will be competent. If a benefic (Jupiter or Venus) be therein, and free from evil aspects, the same effect will accrue. But if the benefic in the 2nd should have good aspects from other planets, then there will be considerable wealth.

Any planet in the 2nd House, badly aspected, will produce difficulty in acquiring money, and if it be a malefic planet which occupies the 2nd House under these conditions, there will be times of stress and even poverty.

Continual hardship and poverty is shown by malefic planets in the 2nd House, in evil aspect to the Moon or Sun; while at the same time the planets in the 2nd House will be severely afflicted by others.

Saturn in the Midheaven afflicting the Sun or Moon is an indication of reversal of fortune, and such persons usually attain considerable position in the world and are then depleted of everything.

Jupiter or Venus in the 10th House, and near the

Financial Prospects

meridian, are signs of good fortune and success in life; and the same results are due to their rising at birth.

In a general manner the aspects to the Moon in a male horoscope or the Sun in a female horoscope should be consulted, and the planets in good aspect thereto will show the means of good fortune, while those in evil aspect will indicate the sources of loss and hurt, according to the Houses the afflicting or assisting planets occupy. Thus Jupiter in good aspect to the Moon from the 11th House shows gain by friends, advisers, and co-operative measures, because the 11th House rules these relationships and Jupiter is the index of increase. Similarly, Uranus in the 7th House would show gain by the marriage partner if in good aspect to the Moon, or loss thereby if in evil aspect.

Mars in the 2nd House shows good earning capacity, because Mars is an ambitious and industrious planet (*i. e.*, it produces such effects in the person), and the 2nd House is the domain of finance. But at the same time it shows extravagance and inability to save money, for Mars is impulsive and lacking thrift.

The 6th House well occupied shows faithful and advantageous servants and employés, such as will augment the fortunes and do good work for the Subject.

Neptune in the 2nd shows complications and an involved state of finance, and frequently it shows loss by fraud and imposition; though in good aspect to other planets it shows gain by such nefarious means. Uranus indicates many ups and downs of fortune, sudden and unexpected rises and falls.

Thus each planet is judged according to its nature and the aspect it throws to the Moon or Sun, while the

Astrology

planets in the 2nd House are judged by their own natures and the aspects which they receive.

Inheritance is shown by a benefic planet in the 5th or 11th House in good aspect to Saturn; but indirect inheritance can be the result of Saturn in good aspect to Jupiter from any part of the figure.

Legacies are shown by good planets, or planets well aspected, in the 8th House; or by Jupiter in good aspect to Uranus from any part of the heavens.

Gain by marriage is shown by benefic planets in the 8th House, because the 8th is 2nd from the 7th, and the 7th House rules over the partner.

The potential of each horoscope is capable of being increased by due attention to the sources of gain, as shown by the position and aspects of the planets in various parts of the heavens; but chiefly by associating oneself with persons whose horoscopes are in harmony with one's own. Thus it happens that individuals are lifted to position and affluence through their association with persons whose horoscopes are in sympathy with theirs. (See Chap. XI. of this Section.)

The Sun and Moon being in good aspect to one another will prevent disaster, or will always provide a means of restoration of fortunes, because it is an index of general good fortune and continual support. Such persons as have this aspect in their horoscopes need never fear misfortune, for if they should fall into disasters in one place, they will always turn up in another with a complete adjustment of their position. But when the Sun and Moon are in evil aspect, and particularly when the malefic planets are in elevation in the heavens, continual misfortune dogs the footsteps, and though there

Financial Prospects

be spells of good fortune, they are brief and attended with troubles.

The benefic planets, Jupiter, Venus, and Sun, being well elevated in the heavens, that is to say, in the 10th or 11th Houses, it is a sign of preponderating good fortune. But when the malefics are in elevation the reverse results happen.

The Line of Least Resistance

It is a law in Nature that the line of least resistance is that of greatest progress. The lightning flash does not come straight to earth, but zigzag by the line of least resistance. The great rivers do not come by a direct course to the ocean, but by many turns and backward reaches, because they follow the path of least resistance. When one comes to take account of the years of human life that are spent in the vain endeavor to achieve the impossible, the lessons of Nature are worth reciting. But what is impossible to one man is facile to another, and the greatest economy of effort is therefore to be secured by proper regard to suitability of occupation and direction of effort.

The principles of Astrology enable us to determine the line of action which at all times will be the most fruitful of results, and in the matter of money-making the matter is decided in the following manner: That planet which has a trine or sextile aspect of the Moon, and is at the same time elevated above the malefic planets, especially if it be itself assisted by the good aspects of other planets, receives first consideration. The House it is in will indicate the source of benefit, but the Sign it is in will show the means through which it will come. Thus if Uranus should be in the Midheaven, in trine aspect to

Astrology

the Moon, and itself receiving a good aspect from either the Sun, Jupiter, or Venus, it will indicate gain through governmental bodies, authorities, and persons of high rank. If Uranus should be in the sign Cancer, it would point to matters associated with the ocean, marine affairs, or those in which water is the element in chief employ; as in marine engineering, shipping, dock building, &c. But if Uranus had been in the 11th House, and in the sign Scorpio, then the source of gain would be by means of companies, syndicates, and associations of a collective nature, and the sign Scorpio would show it to be connected with naval defence (because Scorpio is a martial and watery sign) or the utilisation of waste materials, inflammable oils, &c., or by systems of drainage, which represent the excretory system of a town. By looking chiefly to the nature of the planet concerned, and that of the sign it occupies, a good artist will readily describe the particular line which is to be pursued.

But here, as in every other matter upon which judgment is made, attention must be paid to the character and disposition of the Subject, his aptitudes and qualifications, for it is obviously of little use recommending literature or the law to one whose sole capabilities lie in unintellectual directions. Natural aptitude, supplemented by the necessary training, are the first considerations, for without these success in any direction is but ill assured.

CHAPTER VI

THE POSITION IN LIFE

THIS is to be judged from the position of the majority of the planets, but principally from the Midheaven, the planets therein and its aspects. Thus, if you find the majority of the planets rising, that is to say, in the 10th, 11th, 12th, 1st, 2nd, and 3rd Houses the Subject will be a candidate for responsibility, ambitious of honors and position, and generally independent. If these or the majority of them be well aspected he will become a man of position, employing others; or, if a woman, will hold an important position in her sphere of life, and be esteemed in the social world.

If the degree on the Midheaven receive good aspects from the major planets, the position will be honorable and secure.

Venus or Jupiter, or the Sun well aspected, in the Midheaven, denotes a superior position, honors, and distinction. The same will result if these be rising.

When the majority of the planets are above the horizon, even though they be not rising, the Subject will have responsibilities thrust upon him, even though he should not desire them. If the majority of these planets be well aspected, he will acquit himself creditably and attain to honors.

It is always fortunate for the position that there should be planets exactly on the cusps of either the 2nd, 3rd, 6th, 8th, or 12th Houses, for then there will be every opportunity of securing fame and advancement in life.

But when any of the malefic planets are found exactly on or nearest to the meridian, whether above or below the horizon, there will be loss of position, reversal, a sinister fame, or disgrace.

The 10th House represents the fame and honor of a person, and the 4th House represents the end of life and that which militates against the fame and honor. Therefore when there are good planets in these places, the Subject will meet with rewards and honors commensurate with his efforts; but when evil planets occupy the meridian, he will at best sustain his position in life with great difficulty.

It is futile for any one to suppose that the position of a benefic planet in the meridian of the horoscope will bring him to fame and elevate him in the world irrespective of his own endeavors. The planets operate on human affairs in terms of human thought and action, and that by fixed laws; never adventitiously. That "the Gods help those who help themselves" to the extent that natural laws permit, is a truth which astrology fully provides for. Fitness and fortune are as cause and effect to one another in respect of planetary action in human life.

Many planets in cardinal signs will dispose a man to seek fame, and when the Midheaven of the horoscope is well aspected or there be fortunate planets therein, he

The Position in Life

will attain it. Cardinal signs on the angles of the horoscope (the meridian and horizon), produce fame outlasting death. The same if either of the luminaries be exactly on the equinoxes.

Venus in the Midheaven gives social elevation and lifts a person above the sphere of birth. Good planets in the 11th show patronage.

But when the luminaries are heavily afflicted there will be an inconstant fortune and many reverses, so that position gained will be lost again.

Most of the planets under the horizon shows success and position in the latter part of life, while if they be between the 4th and 7th cusps, there will be advantages after marriage, or by means of partnerships.

In judging of the means by which the position will be sustained, respect must be had to the positions of those planets which are in good aspect to the Midheaven, or to benefic planets in the Midheaven, and if none be so situated, then those which hold benefic aspect to either the Sun or Moon at birth must be taken, and judgment made according to the nature of the planet and the sign it occupies. Preference should always be given to that planet which has the strongest aspect for good. Thus if two planets were in trine, that which is in elevation should be preferred, especially if it be strengthened by the good aspects of other planets.

CHAPTER VII

THE CHOICE OF OCCUPATION

THE enormous waste of force and time entailed by the experimental trip upon which most young men embark at the outset of their career in life, might be greatly reduced by a proper knowledge of individual aptitude in relation to circumstances. The average boy cannot readily make up his mind as to what occupation he will follow, because he does not know either enough of his own powers or of the world in which he is called upon to use them. Parents are in the same difficulty. They must needs wait to see how a boy will shape out. They study his inclinations to the best of their ability, but without coming to a definite conclusion any sooner than the boy himself. Given a fair education, such as may fit him for almost anything, but which specialises him for nothing in particular, he is put to some desk or bench and there left to his own resources. By a fortunate chance, he may find himself suited to his post. More frequently he is several years in finding out that he has missed his vocation, that his inclinations and his work are not in accord, that he has misapplied his energies for some time, and that he has made a false start. Fortu-

The Choice of Occupation

nately circumstanced at birth he may have been equipped by higher education for some distinctive profession, to which he gains access after the payment of large fees or premiums. The man has a strong dramatic faculty and the stage claims him after all. Here is both waste of time and money. Astrology, as a reliable key to character and inclination, deserves some recognition on the grounds of social economy.

The inclinations of the Subject are judged from the position of the majority of the planets, for if they should be found in the aerial signs, Gemini, Libra, or Aquarius, the inclination will be towards mental occupations, especially science and literature. In fiery signs there is a predisposition to a more robust and active life, such as is afforded by military service, travelling, prospecting, exploring, &c. In earthy signs the aptitude lies in the direction of agriculture, experimental science, surveying, dealing in real estate, broking, &c. In watery signs there is special inclination to pursuits connected with the water, such as sailors, watermen, and others; but frequently to other occupation in which fluids are predominant, such as publicans, wine and spirit merchants, chemists, and oil merchants.

Each sign has its special tendency, and the exact occupation can often be decided thereby, when regard is had to the planet in closest aspect to the Sun or Moon and the sign it occupies. Thus Aries denotes soldiers and pioneers of movements; Taurus shows dealers in real estate, house agents and brokers; Gemini, literary men and writers of all sorts; Cancer, sailors and publicans; Leo, actors and artists; Virgo, clothes dealers and sellers of confectionary and bread; Libra, valuers, assayers,

Astrology

money-changers, and pawnbrokers; Scorpio, naval sailors, chemists, dealers in oils and spirits; Sagittarius, explorers, divines, lawyers; Capricornus, political agents and ministers of the State; Aquarius, electricians, company promoters, syndics, and scientific researchers; Pisces, dealers in fish and sea produce, warders, and those connected with places of confinement, such as prisons and hospitals.

Taking, therefore, the dominant planet and the signs that hold the majority of the planets, the line along which the Subject will make the most progress in the world and acquit himself most successfully, may be readily determined.

No person will make a good soldier who has not Mars as a dominant planet, nor will he succeed with the public if the Moon be not elevated and well aspected, nor become a successful artist, musician, or poet if Venus be not conspicuous in the horoscope.

Generally the inclination is derived from a consideration of the dominant planet, and the degree of success attendant upon the occupation is judged from the aspect which that planet throws to the Sun or Moon, and there can be no great advantage from following an inclination which does not promise some measure of success, as is the case when the dominant planet is in evil aspect to the luminaries. Thus it happens that some men follow unprofitable callings, their judgment being dominated by an inclination adverse to their natural welfare. Yet never was good work done in the world without a strong inclination and considerable enthusiasm, and Heaven makes its own slaves, its martyrs, and its scapegoats. And always, the following of an inclination means the

The Choice of Occupation

sacrifice of some of the benefits of life. "Take what thou wilt, but pay the price!" is the Divine mandate, according to Emerson.

But unquestionably, the science which enables a man to choose the line of least resistance, which prevents a youth of intellectual tendencies from wasting the best years of his life in drudgery at the desk or bench, is worth a little study. "Hitch your waggon to a star," is good advice if only we hitch it to the right one.

CHAPTER VIII

MARRIAGE CIRCUMSTANCES

The question as to how, when, and where marriage will take place is an all-absorbing one to the majority of men and women, and no less important than interesting. Astrology has made it possible to answer these questions categorically and with particular precision and verity.

The conditions of connubial life are judged (in a male horoscope) from the condition of the Moon and Venus, and (in a female horoscope) from that of the Sun and Mars. The planet to which the luminary first forms an aspect after birth (that which it "applies" to) denotes the marriage partner. If the aspect be good there will be agreement and the choice of a partner will be fortunate. But if the aspect be evil, there will be trouble after marriage. The nature of the planet to which the luminary forms its aspect after birth ought also to be considered, for if it be that the luminary applies by a good aspect to a benefic planet, or to one that is well-placed and aspected, then there will be considerable happiness and fortune in marriage. On the other hand, if both the aspect and

Marriage Circumstances

the planet be evil—as if the Moon were applying to the opposition of Saturn or Uranus or Mars—then the fate in marriage will be extremely unhappy and disagreements will be frequent and even permanent.

When the aspect and the nature of the planet are at variance, as when the Moon has a good aspect to Saturn, or a bad aspect to Jupiter, there will be a mingled fortune of good and ill in marriage. There is no better sign of happiness and harmony in marriage than a good aspect between the Sun and Moon.

Moreover, it may happen that the Moon applies by good aspect to a planet after birth, and that there is at the same time a malefic body in the 7th House. This indicates that there will be agreement in the connubial life, but that bereavement will soon follow.

When the Moon applies to Neptune there will be some peculiarity or touch of genius in the partner, according as Neptune may be aspected. Uranus shows eccentricity and sometimes wilfulness. Saturn shows steadiness, industry; or jealousy and coldness. Jupiter indicates a good nature, bountiful and honest, but may be given to excess and extravagance. Mars induces industry and practicality, but it gives a strong temper and considerable independence. The Sun shows dignity and loyalty, but may indicate ostentation and foolish pride. Venus denotes peacefulness and a genial, refined nature, but its perversion brings indifference, neglect and disorderliness. Mercury denotes an active and energetic nature, but may produce a busybody and meddler.

Everything depends on the aspect which the significant luminary throws to the planet it applies to, for if the aspect be good it will indicate the better qualities of that

Astrology

planet; but if evil, then there is frequently the unfortunate consequences of choosing a partner in whom the perverted qualities of the planet are predominant.

Good planets in the 7th House indicate a good partner, but when at the same time the aspect of the luminary is evil, it will denote a good marriage, followed by bereavement.

Marriage to a widow (or widower) occurs when Mars and Saturn are the planets concerned in the indications, as if Mars be in the 7th House and in aspect to Saturn, or if the Moon apply to Mars when aspected by Saturn, or when one of them is in the 5th House and the other in the 7th.

Love affairs before marriage are indicated by the 5th House, the planets therein and their aspects, and in a general sense by Venus in a male horoscope and Mars in a female horoscope.

Thus if Venus (or Mars) be afflicted by Saturn or Uranus there will be disappointment in the early affections. Uranus in aspect to Venus gives romantic attachments and much influence over the other sex. Neptune in aspect shows idealism, and when afflicting Venus it produces chaos and entanglement, danger of seduction. Mars afflicting Venus gives ardor and impulse.

More than one Marriage

is indicated when the luminary is in aspect to more than one planet in a double-bodied sign, *e. g.*, Gemini, Sagittarius, or Pisces. Or, if the luminary itself be in a double sign and in aspect to any planet other than one which may be in the 7th House. Also a double sign being on the cusp of the 7th House, and the luminary in a fruitful

Marriage Circumstances

sign, Cancer, Scorpio, or Pisces, or in aspect to planets in those signs. All these are signs of more than one marriage during life.

Signs of separation or divorce are as follows: The luminary applying to the ill aspect of a malefic planet, Venus afflicted, and Uranus in the 7th House or afflicting the Moon or Venus. In female horoscopes change the Significators, taking the Sun and Mars instead of the Moon and Venus, and judge the same.

Where more than one marriage is shown, the ruler of the 7th House denotes the first partner, and the planet ruling the sign it occupies is called its "dispositor" or "displacer." This dispositor represents the second partner.

The planet to which the significant luminary applies is that which is taken to describe the partner, according to the sign it is in. But if this planet be retrograde, *i. e.*, going backwards in the zodiac by apparent motion, then it only represents an attachment which will be broken off. Its dispositor then becomes the significator of the partner. But the ruler of the 7th House is taken for the condition and fortunes of the partner, and if it be afflicted or badly placed and weak in the horoscope, then the marriage will be ill-assorted, unfortunate, and full of dissatisfaction. The contrary is the case when the significant planet is well placed and aspected.

The place or circumstances under which the partner will be met may be known from the sign and house occupied by the planet to which the luminary first applies after birth. Thus if it be in the 11th House, the partner will be met among friends, at the house of a friend, or introduced by a friend. If in the 3rd House, then on a

Astrology

short journey or in correspondence; in the 5th, at a place of amusement; in the 10th, in the course of business; and so on, judgment being made according to the places and circumstances ruled by the House occupied by the planet.

CHAPTER IX

INDICATIONS OF PROGENY

THE 5th House, the planets therein and the position and aspects of the Moon, have to be considered in this matter.

If the 5th House be occupied by benefic planets, or planets well aspected by others, then the progeny will be a source of satisfaction and credit to the Subject, and will be reared to maturity. But the contrary is the case when the 5th House is occupied by malefic planets and such as may be heavily afflicted.

The Moon represents the tendency in the male and the capacity in the female, and when well aspected, or free from evil aspects and well placed, then there will be good fortune in connection with the progeny.

When Uranus afflicts a planet in the 5th House, there will be some premature births, and generally it will be observed that when planets are opposed from the 11th and 5th Houses, or malefic planets occupy those houses, there is trouble through the progeny, and usually the loss of one or more during infancy is to be feared.

Astrology

As to the number of children, no empirical rules exist for the judgment of this matter, which necessarily is a difficult one owing to the fact that we have no means of comparing the horoscopes of man and wife, but the nature of the sign on the cusp of the 5th House is usually to be depended upon for an approximation. Thus Aries, Leo, and Capricornus give small families. Taurus, Cancer, Virgo, Scorpio, and Pisces give large families, and the other signs yield a moderate family. When the Moon is strong, angular, and not afflicted, the number is increased. Twins are born from double-bodied signs occupying the cusp of the 5th House, or planets in the 5th in a double-bodied sign.

The condition of each child is known in a general manner from the alternate Houses, commencing with the 5th. Thus the first child is (in a male horoscope) ruled by the 5th House, and planets therein; the second child by the 7th House; the third by the 9th House, and so on. In a female horoscope the first child is ruled by the 4th House; the second by the 6th House, and so on.

Thus if it be found that there is probability of loss of some of the progeny, the children most liable to affliction may be known by this method; for the Houses which contain the malefic planets, or the afflicted planets, correspond to the afflicted progeny.

Illustrious children are born to the Subject when the ruler of the 5th House is in elevation and well aspected, and in a congenial sign. But if the ruler of the 5th House be badly placed and aspected and in a sign of debility, *i. e.*, opposite to one over which it rules, then the progeny are ill-equipped for the battle of life, either mentally or morally. The particular qualities and

Indications of Progeny

fortunes of the progeny can only be known from their individual horoscopes.

When malefic planets hold the 12th House in a female horoscope, there will be danger in confinement; and the same happens if either of the luminaries, but particularly the Moon, be afflicted in the 5th House.

CHAPTER X

VOYAGES AND JOURNEYS

THE indications of short journeys, inland and around the coast, are to be judged from the 3rd House and the planets therein. If a movable sign be on the cusp of the 3rd House, or planets in a movable sign occupy the 3rd House, then there will be much travelling and many short journeys to and fro. The aspects to these planets in the 3rd will indicate whether such journeys will be mainly successful or not. When there are no aspects to the planet or planets in the 3rd House the fortune of short journeys is to be judged from the nature of the planet in the 3rd, as if Jupiter, they will be fortunate and lucrative; but if Saturn, unfortunate and subject to many hindrances and delays. When malefic planets are afflicted in the 3rd House, or malefic planets in the 3rd throw evil aspects to the Sun or Moon, then there will be dangers and accidents.

Watery signs on the cusp of the 3rd House, or planets in watery signs in the 3rd, indicate cruising and yachting, short journeys by water around the coast. If the Moon be in good aspect to these planets, then there will be safety in passage; but if afflicted by the planets in

Voyages and Journeys

the 3rd there will be danger of collision, capsizing, &c., according to the nature of the planet in the 3rd House.

Long voyages are to be judged in exactly similar manner from the 9th House, the planets therein and their aspects.

The 4th House indicates the place of birth, and if this House hold a benefic planet, or either the Sun or Moon, well aspected, then there is fortune in the place of birth, and journeys should only be undertaken when they are without doubt fortunate in their issues and admit of a return to the native place. When, however, the 4th House is occupied by evil planets or planets heavily afflicted, it will be advisable to remove from the place of birth and seek fortune in more propitious localities.

In this matter the choice is made by reference to that planet which holds the greatest power for good in the horoscope of birth, and the quarter of the Heavens which it occupies will indicate the direction, as from the place of birth, to which the Subject should repair.

Thus, if between the East horizon and the meridian, South-east; between the meridian and the West horizon, South-west; and so of the rest. The points of the compass follow the cardinal points of the Heavens, the Midheaven being South; the Nadir, North; the Ascendant, East; and the Descendant, West. If a malefic planet is rising or setting at birth it is advisable to fix the place of residence so much to the Eastward of the birthplace as will suffice to bring the malefic planets out of the angles of the horoscope. The same if malefic planets occupy the 10th or 4th Houses. On the contrary, if benefic planets are in the 3rd and 9th Houses the Subject should move Westward so as to bring the benefic influences into the 10th and 4th Houses.

Astrology

When benefic planets or planets well aspected occupy the angles of the figure at birth the Subject should not travel far, nor reside long away from the place of birth.

Indications of many voyages are as follows: Many planets in watery signs, Cancer, Scorpio, and Pisces, and also in the sign Virgo. When the majority of the planets are in cardinal and flexed signs, Aries, Gemini, Cancer, Virgo, Libra, Sagittarius, Capricornus, and Pisces, there will be many changes and journeys. Also if the Sun, Moon, Mars, and Mercury are in either the 3rd, 9th, 12th, or 6th Houses, there will be many journeys and long explorations in foreign countries.

When planets are afflicted in watery signs there will be danger in voyages, and if the Moon or Sun be afflicted in Virgo there will be submersion due to wreck.

Also, when there are planets, especially malefics, in Scorpio, Leo, Taurus, and Aquarius, afflicted by the aspects of other planets, or themselves afflicting the Sun or Moon, then there is danger of drowning.

When the signs of voyaging are propitious, and especially when the indications in the 4th House are not so, then removal from the place of birth to some other permanent centre of activity will be advisable. But when good planets or planets well aspected are either rising or in the 4th House, the Subject should remain in his native place, and in the end his patience will be justified.

CHAPTER XI

OF FRIENDS AND ENEMIES

THE general harmony of the horoscope consists in the positions and aspects of the planets and their relations with the luminaries. When this is conspicuous there will be many friends and supporters, and the associations of the Subject will be pleasant and profitable. But when the horoscope is fraught with evil aspects and angular positions of the malefics there will be much strife and many enmities.

In a particular sense the friends and associations of the Subject are to be known from the 11th House and the planets therein. For if there be a benefic planet in the 11th, especially if in good aspect to either of the luminaries, there will be many friends and adherents.

Similarly, the enemies of the Subject are known from the 7th House, and secret enemies from the 12th. Malefic planets therein, especially in evil aspect to the Sun or Moon, shows many opponents.

Neptune in any malefic aspect to the Sun or Moon shows danger of deceit and treachery being practised

Astrology

upon the Subject, and if violent testimonies concur from the ill aspects of Mars or Uranus he will be in danger of an ambush. Saturn in the 7th or 12th shows long feuds and implacable enmities. Uranus therein shows litigation and heckling of creditors. Mars therein is an index of violence and passionate hatred. Mercury therein shows much scandal and many petty annoyances.

Now observe the places of the malefic planets and the Houses wherein they are situated. Take the date when the Sun is in the same longitude as any of these malefic planets, which will be the same in any year, and this will be the birthday of persons who are to be avoided as likely to bring mischief into the life. Supposing, for instance, that Saturn is found at birth in the 10th House, in the 13th degree of the sign Aquarius. Reference to the Ephemeris (Sect. II., chap. i.) will show that the Sun is in Aquarius 13 on the 1st and 2nd February. Hence it would be unfortunate for the Subject to serve any man who was born between the 28th January and the 3rd February in any year. Also, if Uranus were in Leo 23 in the 7th House he should not go into partnership or marriage with anybody born on or near the 15th August in any year.

Take now the places of the benefic planets, and also the place of the Moon, and find the corresponding Solar dates, for these will be the birth dates of such persons as should be cultivated and drawn into close association for mutual benefit.

Observe also the trines and sextiles of the benefic planets and of the Moon, and the squares and opposi-

Of Friends and Enemies

tions of the malefics, for these will operate in a minor degree in a similar manner as already indicated.

A comparison of the horoscopes of persons, whether kings or plebeians, with those of others who have wrought great good or evil in their lives, will immediately establish this observation. Indeed there is nothing more dependable in the whole range of scientific observation than this sympathy and antipathy of horoscopes and their corresponding results. It is an argument for the claim of its advocates that Astrology should be regarded in the light of a science, for if the planets act not at all upon the dispositions and tendencies of men their squares and oppositions in two separate horoscopes would have no signification. Let those who are unhappily mated compare their horoscopes and they will find the signs of discord to which reference has been made above. On the other hand, let any man who has been lifted to wealth, fame, or position by the patronage of another compare his horoscope with that of his benefactor, and it will be found that the benefic planets in the latter hold the places of the Sun, Moon, Midheaven, or Ascendant in his own. This frequently accounts for the fact that men with comparatively unfortunate horoscopes are sometimes found in positions of influence and in the enjoyment of considerable fortune. The complex fabric of life has its warp and woof wherein many colored threads are woven together for the completing of the grand design, and the great loom of life has its wheels within wheels which only the Great Artificer can understand and regulate. We here below, subjects all of interplanetary action, must content ourselves with the design as re-

Astrology

vealed to us in the history of mankind, or we must seek to understand the purpose of life, its motif, the complex laws which operate to bring about the unfoldment of the great plan, and thence to prognosticate that which hereafter shall be revealed to the commonplace observer.

CHAPTER XII

THE END OF LIFE

THE end of life is judged from the planets occupying the 8th and 4th Houses, for the 8th denotes Death, and the 4th denotes the final resting-place of man. When benefic planets, or the Luminaries well aspected, occupy these Houses, you may judge that the end will be peaceful, normal, and that death will take place in the midst of congenial and even exceptionally agreeable surroundings.

When, however, the malefic planets hold these Houses, or afflict the luminaries therein, you may judge greater stress and privation.

Uranus in the 8th House denotes a sudden death, and the same result is observed when the Luminaries therein are afflicted by Uranus. Neptune in the 8th denotes danger of trance, coma, and simulated death, and when this position is observed it is necessary that all the signs of mortification should be present before interment is effected. Saturn produces death by privation and obstructions, by chills and colds. Mars induces death by fevers and inflammatory action, and frequently by hæmorrhage.

Astrology

Planets in Fixed signs in the 8th House show death from heart or throat affections, affections of the excretory system and the blood. In Cardinal signs, the head, stomach, kidneys, or skin are the seats of the fatal disease. In Flexed signs, the lungs, bowels, and nervous system become fatally affected.

Violent or unnatural deaths are shown when either of the luminaries is simultaneously afflicted by the evil aspects of more than one of the malefic planets, or when both luminaries are separately afflicted by the malefic aspects of malefic planets, Neptune, Uranus, Saturn, or Mars.

When these testimonies occur, it will be found that Neptune produces death by assassination, Uranus by sudden catastrophies, explosions, hurts by electricity and machinery, Saturn by blows and falls, and Mars by cuts, burns, scalds, and effusion of blood. Particular judgment is drawn from the nature of the signs in which the significant planets are placed. Thus Saturn in Watery signs would produce drowning; in Taurus, strangling or decapitation; in Aries by the blow of a truncheon, &c. Similarly, Uranus in Gemini would produce accidents on short journeys, railway collisions, bicycle or motor accidents, and the like effects. It is impossible to cite all the effects due to the several planets in the different signs, but if the simple natures of the planets, signs and Houses are thoroughly understood, a combination of their significations will readily lead to an appreciation of exact effects. If I say that a certain fluid is H_2SO_4, any one having a knowledge of elementary chemistry will know that it is sulphuric acid, and similarly, if I say that a certain horoscope contains Saturn in Cancer in

The End of Life

the 3rd, which is astrologically expressed ♄ ♋ 3, any one who has read the first pages of this book with attention will be able to say: Let the Subject beware of short journeys by water! It is all chemistry of a kind.

When the 4th House contains benefic planets, or planets that throw good aspects to the luminaries, there will be peace and comfort in old age, or in the end of life whensoever it may be determined. Neptune therein shows retirement and sequestration, and when afflicting the luminaries or itself afflicted, it denotes death in an asylum, hospital, or other place of detention. Uranus in the 4th, in similar conditions, denotes a sudden and remarkable death. Saturn similarly placed and aspected shows death in exile, privation or great trouble. Mars in the 4th House afflicting the luminaries or itself afflicted by other adverse planets, denotes a violent death by gunshot or wound and in the midst of strife, or on the field of battle.

Before any catastrophic death be predicted, it should be carefully decided whether or not the death is compassed with uncommon and violent indications, not that one need have fear of the mere going out or coming into the world, but there is some choice of gates, and rather than affright the weak-minded with a sinister judgment, it is better to leave them to find their own way.

SECTION IV

THE STARS IN THEIR COURSES

CHAPTER I

THE TIME-MEASURE

The planets, in their motions after birth, come into certain relations with the planets in the horoscope of birth, and also form aspects among themselves owing to the diversities of their motions in the Zodiac. In Astrological science there are two separate means of calculating the time of events, but both methods consist of bringing the body of one planet to the body or aspect of another, which process is called "Directing," and the arc described by the moving body is called an "Arc of Direction."

The first of these methods is the discovery of Claudius Ptolemy, the famous mathematician and geographer, the author of the Syntaxis, as set forth in his work the Tetrabiblos, or Four Books on the influence of the Stars. This method had the support and confirmation of the

The Time-Measure

great Kepler. It has respect to the rising, setting, and meridian passage of the planets after birth, whereby they are brought to the places or aspects of the planets in the Radix (the Root), which is the horoscope of birth.

The limits and nature of this work do not permit of a thorough exposition of this method, which entails some little knowledge of spherical trigonometry, but the reader who desires to perfect himself therein is referred to the author's work, entitled "Prognostic Astronomy." A facile application of the method is here given, by which any one may, by the aid of the Tables of Houses, make certain of the more important calculations by rule of thumb, and predict thence the times of remarkable events.

The principle involved is this: The number of degrees which pass over the meridian between the moment of birth and the rising or culminating of a planet, will equal the number of years which must elapse from birth until the influence of that planet becomes dominant.

Thus, if Jupiter at birth is coming to the meridian, that is to say, if it be in the 10th, 11th, or 12th House, count the number of degrees between the meridian and Jupiter, and in so many years from the time of birth there will be an access of good fortune. Similarly, if Saturn or other of the malefic planets be coming to the meridian, the number of degrees between it and the Midheaven will indicate the age at which troubles will abound.

Also, when the planets have passed the meridian, the measure is made in the same way, by bringing the Midheaven to the place of the planet, counting the degrees between the planet and Midheaven for the number of years at which it will operate.

Astrology

But the same and other planets may be directed to the horizon, by taking the Table of Houses for the latitude of the birthplace (Sect. I., chap. iii.) and finding therein under the column marked "Ascen." (Ascendant) the longitude held by any of the planets. Observe then what degree is on the Midheaven in the column marked 10 (10th House), and count the number of degrees between this Midheaven and the Midheaven at birth. The result will give the age at which the effects of such planets will be experienced.

Thus, for a person born in or near Liverpool or in the same latitude, suppose the Midheaven at birth to be in Scorpio 0, and Saturn to be in the 2nd House in Aquarius 8 degrees. I wish to bring Saturn to the horizon. In the Table of Houses I find that Aquarius 8 is on the Ascendant when Sagittarius 9 is on the Midheaven, and I therefore count from Scorpio 0 to Sagittarius 9. This gives the age of 39 years, and as Saturn is in the 2nd House at birth, I say that at 39 years of age the Subject would experience financial disaster, and because Saturn comes then to the Ascendant, I also say there would be serious illness and depression of spirits.

When planets are setting at birth they are brought to the opposition of the Ascendant in a similar manner, only the opposite point of the zodiac must be found in the Tables under the Ascendant. Thus, if Mars were in the 7th House at birth in the 11th degree of Cancer, I find the opposite point (Capricornus 11) under the column of the Ascendant, and I note that Scorpio 19 is then on the Midheaven, so that from Scorpio 0 to Scorpio 19 gives 19 years, at which age the Subject would have a serious illness due to inflammatory action in the stomach and

The Time-Measure

probably produced by overwork and worry, as indicated by the sign Cancer and the planet Mars, or if there be indications of an accident, then an accident by scalding with hot water or acids would be predicted.

Planets are brought to the opposition of the Midheaven by counting the degrees which intervene between the longitude on the lower meridian at birth and that held by the planet.

In all such directions the conjunctions of benefic planets are advantageous when directed to the Midheaven or Ascendant, and the conjunctions of the malefics are indicated of periods of bad fortune. The oppositions are uniformly evil, whether the planet involved in the direction be a benefic or malefic. (Sect. I., chap. iv.)

These are the directions of the planets to the two Significators, the Midheaven and Ascendant. The Midheaven appertains to honors and credit, while the Ascendant has relation to the personal and bodily welfare and the general fortunes.

To direct the Midheaven or Ascendant to the other aspects of the planets, such as the sextile, trine, semi-square or square, it is only necessary to note the degrees in which these aspects fall and bring them to the Midheaven or Ascendant as if the body of the planet were itself there, and in the manner already indicated.

The Sun is directed after birth by its motion in the zodiac, which can be found in the Ephemeris for the year of birth, and the aspects it forms to the planets in the horoscope and in the daily progress should be tabulated. In most Ephemerides they are already calculated, so that the labor is considerably lightened. Each day after birth will represent one year of life, the

Astrology

mean motion of the Sun being about 1 degree per day. All that is necessary, therefore, is to count the number of days from birth to the date when the Sun forms an aspect, and that will give the age at which the planet aspected will produce its effects.

As the Sun goes through the zodiac the other bodies make progress along with it, in which course they form aspects to the Midheaven, Ascendant, the Sun and Moon in the horoscope of birth. These are called "Secondary" directions, and in connection with the Sun's aspects after birth, constituted the system in use among the Arabian astrologers.

Minor periods of good and bad fortune, subsidiary to the above periodic influences, are taken from the Moon's progress after birth, in which one day equals one year of life, and two hours equal one month. These directions of the Moon afford a monthly prognosis of the course of events, and are useful in the conduct of minor affairs in life. When they are contrary to the general trend and import of the periodic directions made to the Midheaven, Ascendant, and Sun, they act indifferently, and frequently produce only passing benefits or annoyances; but when they are in agreement with the Primary Directions cited above, then they accentuate and define the nature and time of events. As if the Primaries be good and the Lunar directions evil, then there will be a predominance of good fortune with some current disturbances; but both being good there will be abundant success and satisfaction; while if the Primaries be evil and the Lunar directions good, the latter will serve only to moderate the effects for the time being of the Primary evil indications.

The Time-Measure

An intelligent apercu of the principles of directing will greatly enhance the value of any prognostications made from the horoscope of birth, as it will enable the student to select those periods in the life when the effects due to any planet are most likely to eventuate. Thus, if Saturn be in the 2nd House at birth, it may be said that there would follow some periods of great financial stress, and the rising of Saturn by direction after birth would show the time when one, at all events, of such periods would be experienced.

And here is the great fact upon which astrologers the world over are prepared to stand or fall. If the planets have no effect in the lives of men, their directions to the angles of the horoscope can have no effect; but never was it found that a man had evil fortunes at the period when the planet Jupiter was directed to the Midheaven or Ascendant, or anything but bad fortune when Saturn was similarly directed. The fact is there, and we cannot get away from it. The only question is as to how far we can intelligently carry our investigations beyond that point, and intelligibly convey our discoveries to the world by their application to the affairs of daily life. The reader may judge for himself from a perusal of these pages.

The directions being calculated and tabulated in order of their occurrence, the time and general nature of the influences operating in successive periods of the life will stand revealed. The particular nature of the events indicated by the several directions may be known from (a) the House in which the directed planet is situated; (b) the Sign it occupies; and (c) the aspect it forms, considered in relation to the nature of the planet. For

Astrology

example: If Uranus at birth were in the 9th House and the sign Gemini, its direction to the Midheaven would be the index of litigation in connection with writings, publications, or means of transit; because the 9th House, among other things, has relation to litigation and legal affairs, and Gemini (the 3rd House sign) to communications, writings, &c., while Uranus denotes sudden and unexpected events, ruptures, alienations, and complexities.

So if Saturn were in the 6th House in the sign Aquarius, its direction to the opposition of the Ascendant would indicate chills to the blood, anemia, &c., constituting a serious illness with probability of low fever; because the 6th House rules sickness, and Aquarius rules the blood, while Saturn is the cause of chills, paucity, and impediments.

Thus the time and nature of events may be known with great certainty.

CHAPTER II

THE EFFECTS OF TRANSITS

AMONG the number of important indicators to which Astrologers refer in making a forecast of concurrent events, there are the transits of the planets over the places of the Significators at birth, the positions of Eclipses, and those of the lunations.

The first of these chronocrators depends upon the revolutions of the planets in their orbits. Each planet has a period in which it completes its revolution in the heavens, in the course of which it passes the places of the Sun, Moon, Midheaven, and Ascendant of the horoscope. This passage over the radical Significators is technically termed its "transit," and it will be found that such transits afford a very precise and reliable source of prognostication, for the time of a planet's transit is known in advance of its occurrence (see Sect. II., chap. iv.), and the effects of such transit are in exact terms of the nature of the planet concerned. It is only necessary to add that the Midheaven and the Sun have relation to the position and honor of the Subject, while the Moon and Ascendant have relation to the personal health and general fortunes. The Sun

Astrology

and Midheaven also signify the father, and the Moon has general signification of the mother. Venus signifies domestic and love affairs, the affections and sentiments; while Mercury signifies the mental disposition. So Uranus in transit over the place of Venus will give a love affair, a romantic attachment. Mars over the place of Venus will engender passionate love. Saturn over Venus will give disappointment or bereavement; and Neptune thereover will bring entanglements and complications, with danger of being led astray. Saturn over Mercury will produce melancholy and many errors of judgment. Mars over the same planet will excite the mind and dispose to impulse and unreasoning anger, quarrels and disputation. Uranus over Mercury will render the mind wayward and headstrong, disposed to erratic courses and egotistic methods. Neptune passing the place of Mercury produces deceits, treacheries, and apprehension of impending evil, a sense of espionage and ambush. It involves the mind in tortuous and complicated schemes, and disposes to secrecy and weariness.

The transits of the major planets are of chief significance, and their effects are rendered more weighty and lasting when at the time of transit they are retrograde in the zodiac; while their stationary positions on the places of the Significators have almost the same power as Primary Directions.

Of Eclipses

An Eclipse of the Sun or Moon falling on the place of any Significator in the horoscope of birth is of a sinister import, and cannot be too seriously considered. Falling

The Effects of Transits

on the Ascendant or the Moon they affect the health and general fortunes very seriously, and only a series of subsequent good directions can avail to restore the Subject to his normal condition. On the Midheaven or the Sun, the honor and fortunes may both be affected, and in the same serious degree. The Eclipses falling on the places of the other planets will produce effects in accord with the nature of those planets and the Houses they occupy. To have any appreciable effect, the Eclipses must be within two degrees of any of the radical positions, or of their opposition aspects.

Of Lunations

The Lunations recur in the same part of the Ecliptic every nineteen years. Considered in relation to the current indications they afford the means of a monthly forecast of events. Thus, if the lunation for the month falls on the place of Jupiter in the horoscope of birth, it will produce good effects in that department of life which is governed by the House in which Jupiter is situated; as if in the 11th, through friends; in the 4th, through property or rental; in the 6th, through servants and health; in the 8th, through a financial colleague, &c.

The effects of Lunations are subsidiary to the current lunar directions, and these in turn are subsidiary to the transits, and the transits to the Primary Directions. By this it is not meant that they are inoperative, nor that they fail to indicate the events of the month, but their power and degree of influence is subject to the greater influence of superior causes. And as a general observation it may be affirmed that the less frequently any celestial position occurs in a horoscope, the greater is its

Astrology

influence. This fact gives to primary directions their great influence in the life, for they can only occur once in a lifetime; and for the same reason Eclipses have a major significance, for the same Eclipse only recurs after an interval of 649 years. The transits of Neptune, of Uranus, of Saturn and Jupiter and Mars follow in their order of frequency. Neptune has a revolution of about 165 years, Uranus 84 years, Saturn 30 years, Jupiter 12 years, and Mars 1¼ years.

Major effects must not therefore be referred to inferior causes, and minor effects must not be referred to superior causes. In universal or even national cataclysms, individual fortunes are submerged.

CHAPTER III

HOW TO SUMMARISE A HOROSCOPE

BEFORE leaving the exposition of this subject, it may be of advantage to the reader if I give some idea of the method to be pursued in the complete handling of a horoscope.

First, then, erect the figure of birth, taking care to use the Ephemeris of the year of birth, and also the correct Table of Houses for the latitude of the place of birth.

Next proceed to attempt a description of the chief personal traits of the Subject, following in succession with a well-considered judgment on the constitution, hereditary tendencies, the health and pathological predispositions, the mental traits and disposition, considering these latter in relation to the state of health indicated. Then pass to a consideration of the environing conditions of life; the financial condition and outlook; the position in life; the occupation; prospects and conditions of marriage; of progeny. Judge next concerning voyages and journeys. Finish with a statement regarding the predominance of friends or enemies, and select dates by Solar positions, as already instructed.

Astrology

In cases where it is not objected to, an approximation may be made to the time and nature of death.

Throughout the whole of this judgment, the periods when these predicted effects will come into force should be made by reference to the rising, setting, and meridian passage of the planets, the solar aspects, and transits.

Care should be taken to weigh justly and impartially the evidence set before you in the figure of the heavens for birth. Major importance should be given to those planets which are in angles, and those which are in elevation, for the nearer a planet may be to the Midheaven, the greater is its influence for good or ill, according to its nature and aspect.

Read what you see, not what you imagine should be the destiny of an individual. If you are in complete ignorance of his person, position, and environment, so much the better. If you follow carefully the various rules which are contained in this book, you may at first make some errors of judgment, but as you become familiar with the task, even these errors will become few and far between, and in the end the language of the horoscope will become so intelligible and clear that it will interpret itself, and the whole trend and potentiality for good or ill of any birth-figure will force itself upon you in just the same way as when a man walks into your presence with his character clearly stamped upon his face, so that you have only to look and know.

Having become proficient in the judgment of birth-figures, you will do well to proceed to a closer study of the mathematics of astrology, making yourself proficient in the various methods of directing, so that you may at

How to Summarise a Horoscope

any time refine upon your general prognostics, and make predictions which are clear, sharp, and to the point.

Undoubtedly there is a modicum of intuitive perception at work in the judgment of any horoscope, which will enable you to seize upon the small details and exact pointing of any matter, and this perhaps constitutes the whole difference between the rule of thumb worker and the inspirational reasoning of the intuitive worker. The one exhausts the books and the other embellishes them. It is so with science in every department. The books will take you up to a certain point of proficiency, and a strict regard for the formulæ will keep you within the bounds of safety. But if you are ever to make a discovery or become a recognised exponent of any science, you must be naturally gifted with what is called the "scientific imagination," another name for intuition. But at no point does true intuition part company with exact reasoning. There is no lesion. The one is an extension of the other. It is the higher reason, which argues from the known to the unknown. And the Astrologer is in this respect as the poet, "born, not made." But a moment's reflection will suffice to convince you that the more facile you may become with the book-learning and technique of Astrology, the more you will leave the intuition free to act. When a lad is struggling with his multiplication tables, his appreciation of the binomial theorem or the differential calculus cannot be said to amount to much. And, in the same way, a person who is stuffing down the Alphabet of Astrology cannot be expected to intuite anything concerning the potential of the Sun's direction to the quadrature of Saturn.

CHAPTER IV

HOW TO BECOME A SUCCESSFUL ASTROLOGER

I TAKE it that nobody nowadays can afford to fritter away time in the study of subjects which are not likely to become a source of benefit to himself and others. If there be such people among my readers, which I consider unlikely, I may dismiss them offhand with the remark that they will never become successful astrologers, for the first word of practical astrology is Utility. If the science had not its practical application to the affairs of everyday life, if its principles contained no word of assurance and hope for the myriad toilers of this world, no word of admonition for the self-indulgent parasites of modern social life, if, in short, it did not make for the betterment of human life and thought, it would never have attracted the attention of Aristotle, Cicero, Galen, Claudius Ptolemy, Thales, and others of the old world, and such men as Bacon, Cordan, Archbishop Usher, Naibod, Mercator, Ashmole, Kenelm Digby, Sir Christopher Heydon, Dryden, Dr. John Butler, Sir George Wharton, Vincent Wing, George Witchel, Tycho Brahe, Kepler, and Flamstead of more recent biography. Indeed, in whatever age or country we may elect to make

A Successful Astrologer

our inquiries concerning Astrology, there are to be found a host of intelligent and even illustrious advocates in every department of life and learning. Suffice it to say that the modern student of this most ancient of all sciences is at all times in very good company.

Let it first be understood that there is an object to be attained in the study of Astrology, and that the pursuit of it in the gratification of an idle curiosity alone will inevitably entail the waste of time which invariably attaches to idleness of all descriptions, and we may then profitably consider whether or not the subject is worth the labor which it will demand from the man who has something to do in the world and little enough time in which to do it. These are stressful times, and we have to be economical in our efforts. We have strength enough to carry us through, but neither strength enough to thresh the wind nor time enough to fish in puddles.

What, then, does Astrology offer to the patient worker, the man who would become a successful Astrologer?

First and foremost it will enable him to gain an insight into individual motive and character which no other science can possibly afford. It will enable him to know himself, his own strength and weakness, and so fit him to deal harmoniously and justly with others. It will enhance his opportunities to the extent that he is able to foresee and make use of all benefic influences operating through his own environment. It will give him timely warning of his approach to the quicksands and pitfalls which occur in his passage through life. He will discern his special weaknesses, and the times of his predisposition to sickness, the nature thereof, and

Astrology

the precautions which are necessary. He will know whom to cultivate and whom to avoid, and in selecting a partner in business or a wife for his home, he will be guided by a foreknowledge of evils to be avoided and of good things to be gained. He will choose his path in life with the confidence that it is for him the line of least resistance and therefore that of greatest progress. He will not become obsessed by ambitions beyond his power to achieve. He will learn the power of adaptation to environment, and thereby effect his work in the world with the least possible friction and waste of force. He will know when to make provision against sickness, accident, and death. He will not invest capital where interest is not to be gained. He will see the end from the beginning. It may not make him a brilliant success in the world, but it will assuredly save him from being a failure. He will find causes for inexplicable things, and his mind will rest content in the knowledge that while he is working out the highest potentialities of his own horoscope, the major problems and intricacies of life are not of his making or needful of his solving. And finally, when his time comes to "shuffle off this mortal coil," he will be prepared, and will know that it is the will of Heaven, expressed and determined from the moment of his birth. Rightly employed, Astrology cannot fail to improve the man who makes of it a serious study, fitting him to be of greater use to others and of higher service to the race at large.

But to become a successful Astrologer he must study patiently for several years, testing each statement that is made in the books by reference to his own and several other horoscopes. He must be able to erect a figure of

A Successful Astrologer

the Heavens with mathematical accuracy for any given time and place, work out directions by the use of the sphere or trigonometrical tables, and have a competent knowledge of the motions and periods of the various planetary bodies. When thus satisfied in his own mind that Astrology is a dependable science, and that he is capable of demonstrating it under test conditions, he must be generous in the use of it. Here and there he will find one who is opposed to the belief that the stars have any influence in human affairs. Let him not waste logic with such a man, but go straight to the task of convincing him by an appeal to facts.

For preference, select a period when the directional influences are such as seem likely to hit the sceptic with considerable force, define the event, make a careful calculation of the time of its fulfilment, and put them on paper, which, being yet unread by the man of Common-sense, should be placed under cover, sealed, and endorsed to be opened only after a certain date.

Now a man who has been hammered rather severely and in quite an unexpected manner, is usually open to conviction of truth when he finds that the nature and date of his disaster have been accurately foretold. Being a man of "common-sense" and not of intuition, he will probably think that the Astrologer might even have saved him from the consequences of his own lack of foresight. So indeed might the Astrologer have done had he taken the management of affairs from the beginning; but to step in half-way to arrest causes which are already in operation and charged with inevitable effects, is requiring too much of any man short of a Prime Minister!

There are certain things which even the most astute

Astrology

deductive reasoner cannot foresee, and these are the points that should be utilised by the Astrologer who seeks to convince others of the truth of his science. A man cannot reason from his doorstep to a street accident. If he could he would avoid it. All men are not subject to accidents, however. But almost all are subject to bereavements, losses, sicknesses, and changes of fortune. Those are the points which the Astrologer intent on proselytising, usually makes use of. But events need not be in futurity to carry conviction. If it can be shown that by mathematical calculations the events of the past can be recited with precision and exactness, it is evident to the meanest intellect that nothing hinders from an extension of such calculations into the future. And once convinced of the reliability of such claims to foreknowledge, the practical man of the world is not slow to avail himself of its uses.

But Astrology is not exhausted in the study of individual horoscopes, for there are other departments of this extensive science. The influence of the planets upon the weather, as embodied in Astro-meteorology; the rise and fall of Empires, political changes, the outbreak of wars, of revolutions, of epidemics, as defined by State Astrology so much in repute among the Oriental rulers; the occurrence of tidal waves, earthquakes, and other seismic phenomena, all form a part of the complete equipment of the practical Astrologer.

It would be superfluous to recite here the numerous and strikingly accurate forecasts which have been made by modern exponents of the science, but it is only right to say that they reflect considerable credit upon their authors, for the above-mentioned departments of astro-

A Successful Astrologer

logical learning are by no means in the same efficient state as Genethliacal Astrology, to an outline of which this work is devoted. Anciently it was otherwise, and even in the East at this day they hold some secrets of traditional knowledge, concerning which they are unduly mysterious and of which we have only the evidence afforded by more exact prediction upon certain points.

Prejudice and Ignorance are the twin giants which bar the path of the world's progress to-day, even as they have ever done. Step by step they have been beaten back, baffled by the light of Reason, harassed by the arrows of Truth. The world is redeeming its ancient heritage. All that is now required to establish the paramount truth of Astrology as a science is an impartial and thorough investigation, preferably at the hands of scientific men, of its methods and principles. Not that the truth is to be ratified at the hands of modern scientists, seeing that their own teaching constitutes a mere shifting orthodoxy, liable at any moment to undergo a fundamental change in theory by the discovery of a single new fact—but that to such men rightly belongs the duty of disproving the claims of Astrology to be considered as a science, for it is a fact to be regretted that certain members of their body have written against the subject in a spirit of prejudice and without adducing any data in support of their contention, which ill becomes any man of scientific pretensions and is above all things detrimental to the cause of Truth.

CHAPTER V

A POPULAR ILLUSTRATION

IN order to summarise and illustrate the principles which have been enunciated in the course of this work, I shall avail myself of the horoscope of Mr. Joseph Chamberlain, who was born on the 8th of July, 1836, at Highbury, the time of birth being stated to have been at about 2.30 in the morning. Calculations have since enabled us to fix the exact time of birth as at 2 h. 36 m. a.m. I subjoin the horoscopical figure for that time, the calculation of which is as follows:—

	H.	M.	S.
Midheaven in R.A. at Noon 7th July, 1836..	7	1	58
Add time elapsed since....................	14	36	0
Equation for 14h. 33m. at 10secs.		2	25
Midheaven in Right Ascension at Birth.....	21	40	23

The Constitution

Born under the sign Gemini, with Mercury rising in the sign Cancer, the Sun near the conjunction with Jupiter and in close sextile to the Moon, there is little

A Popular Illustration

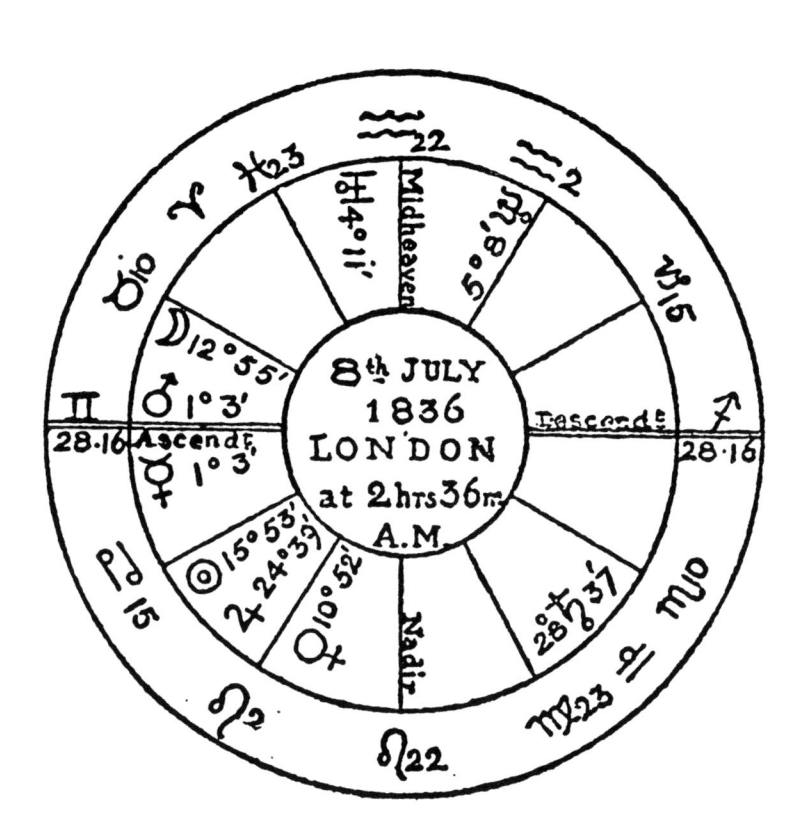

Astrology

doubt that the late Colonial Secretary is by nature gifted with an excellent constitution. The sextile of the luminaries is a powerful co-ordinator, and whenever sickness supervenes there will be a speedy recovery. The semi-square aspect of Mars, while disposing to gouty affections of the hands and feet, will contribute vital energy and power to throw off diseases, while at the same time predisposing to accidents and wounds to the right shoulder or clavicle.

The rising sign gives nervous energy and enormous capacity for work, which is due to high nervous tension supported by a sound vitality. The only hereditary predisposition is that indicated by Mars, which induces to fevers, and gouty affections due to acidity.

The Health

The Moon is strong in the sign Taurus, but not particularly well placed in the 12th House. It has, moreover, the square aspects of Neptune and Venus from fixed signs. These indications point to functional disorders of the heart, throat, and excretory system. On the other hand, there are the good aspects of the Sun, Jupiter, and Uranus to counteract these adverse tendencies, and it is certain that strong recuperative powers together with a normally good co-ordination of functions would induce a speedy recovery from any illness to which he may be liable. Considerable immunity from sickness of all sorts may therefore be predicated.

Character and Disposition

The majority of the planets being in Cardinal signs, with three planets (including the Moon) in Fixed signs,

A Popular Illustration

indicates a character that is energetic, ambitious, active, sharp, ingenious, lively, and persevering; capable of cutting out a line in life for himself and making headway against obstacles; disposed to ride roughshod over the weaknesses and prejudices of those who oppose him; gifted with a pioneer spirit, incisive manner, and disposed at times to effect his ends regardless of the feelings and opinions of others. At the same time there is sufficient patience, method, caution, and watchfulness to make this extreme definition of purpose very effective. Laborious, firm (at times obstinate), systematic, and self-reliant, he is capable of waiting for opportunities. But finally he carries his purpose with a *tour de force*.

That which he lacks is adaptability, suavity, and ability to enter into the feelings of others. He is too ambitious to be self-centred, but yet too intent to be sympathetic.

The rising of Mercury in trine aspect to Saturn and Uranus gives considerable mental capacity, a wide grasp of facts, a well-informed, apt and business-like mind; some originality, constructiveness, and power of marshalling facts and figures; patience, caution, and secrecy. There is not much imagination, and the sympathies are not wide. His methods and actions are governed by literal fact and mathematical certainty. He is an omnivorous devourer of the accessible. He takes the small fish by the handful and makes a meal of them; but he leaves the ponderous whales for those of greater imagination and more leisurely habit.

The quadrature of Mars to Uranus will induce momentary outbursts of temper and some irritability of nature, but the character I am delineating is not such

Astrology

as can easily be played upon, for it is remarkably lacking in emotional susceptibility. Nevertheless, the inspirational faculty is by no means absent, and the presence of Neptune in the 9th House in trine to the rising Mercury, is an index of considerable inventive genius, extreme range of mental perception, and telescopic discernment of future events. Venus in the 3rd House shows some artistic tastes and fancies, considerable appreciation of art and culture, a fondness for flowers, bright lights, &c. But dominant above all are the two angular influences of Uranus and Mercury, which render the mind mathematical and precise, commercial, apt, business-like, energetic, and eminently magnetic.

Finance

The position of the Sun in conjunction with Jupiter in the sign Cancer, in sextile to the Moon, is the index of a high fortune and means exceeding a competence. It is here worthy of note that Cancer, which in this horoscope holds the Sun, Jupiter, and Mercury, is the ruling sign of South Africa, with which Colony Mr. Chamberlain's fortunes have been for a long time so intimately associated. It is also worthy of note that both Cecil Rhodes and Barney Barnato were born on the same day of the year, the 5th of July, with the Sun in the 14th degree of Cancer. In the former case the Sun was conjoined with Moon and Venus, in sextile to Uranus and trine to Neptune, while in the latter case the Sun was in trine to Jupiter. In regard to Mr. Chamberlain's horoscope, it will be observed that Jupiter, which holds such effective power for increase in the 2nd House, is also the ruler of the 7th, and it is to be remembered that all partnerships,

A Popular Illustration

commercial or social, which he has contracted have so far proved highly satisfactory from a merely monetary point of view. Further, the Moon is affected with the good aspect of the Sun in the 2nd House, which is a further indication that on a purely financial basis Mr. Chamberlain is a man worth going into partnership with.

Position

All the planets except Neptune and Saturn are rising, and this at once indicates a man ambitious of independence and honors, one who is confessedly a candidate for responsibility.

Uranus in the Midheaven and close to the meridian indicates that association with civic and governmental bodies in which Mr. Chamberlain has rendered himself so conspicuous a figure, and whereas the trine aspect of Mercury in the Ascendant to Uranus in the Midheaven and the sextile of the Moon to Uranus also are sure indications of a wide popularity, the square aspect of Mars to Uranus from the 12th House, will not fail to engender many veiled enmities, machinations, and inimical plots, which have for their object the overthrow of Mr. Chamberlain's prestige, and which, failing, will find expression in vituperative abuse and bitter animosity. But those who understand the virtue of the orientality of planets in a horoscope will retain their confidence in Mr. Chamberlain's ability to hold his own against all opponents.

It will be observed that the direction of the Ascendant to the place of Uranus in the horoscope coincides with the age of Mr. Chamberlain at the outbreak of hostilities in South Africa, while the direction of Midheaven opposi-

Astrology

tion Saturn coincides with the progress of the Boer War. Did space permit it would be possible to adduce a long list of directional arcs coinciding with the time and nature of all the more important epochs in Mr. Chamberlain's career. The student is invited to make some test of this matter by the aid of the rules already given in these pages.

Marriage

Mr. Chamberlain has been thrice married. It will be observed that not only is there a double-bodied sign on the cusp of the 7th House, but the Moon also applies to both the Sun and Jupiter in the sign Cancer. (See Sect. III., chap. 8.) The aspect of the Moon being benefic to both the Sun and Jupiter, the marital state would be both harmonious and fortunate. It is, of course, well known that Mr. Chamberlain has, from a merely worldly point of view, married most advantageously. This observation may be called "wise after the event," but I would observe that this geniture preceded my judgment of it, and the rules from which I judge are to be found in the Tetrabiblos of Ptolemy, written in the second century, and since tested and found reliable by successive astrologers during some seventeen centuries. Saturn's aspect to Jupiter, the ruler of the 7th House, and the Moon's quadrature to Venus must be held accountable for the successive bereavements which have disturbed the conjugal life in this case.

Progeny

The position of Saturn in the 5th House, and the affliction of Venus by Neptune and the Moon, will serve to account, in connection with the marriage conditions,

A Popular Illustration

for the small family which has been born to Mr. Chamberlain, for observe that Venus is the ruler, jointly with Mercury, of the 5th House, while Saturn is in the 5th and ruler of the 8th House. The same positions and aspects threaten to curtail the succession.

The position of Mercury, joint ruler of the 5th, in the sign Cancer, and just about to rise in the horoscope, promises honors and distinctions to the first-born.

Travelling

The Moon and Mars are cadent in the Horoscope, and Mercury, the "winged messenger" (symbol of the trading-ship), is rising. These are indications of many journeys and changes and constant unrest. But fixed signs being on the cusps of the 3rd and 9th Houses, and the Moon also in a fixed sign, will suffice to account for the fact that Mr. Chamberlain is not a great long-distance traveller. Cancer and Leo holding the benefics and the Sun also well aspected in Cancer, the Moon being in Taurus, shows at once that France, South Africa, Holland, Scotland, and Ireland are parts of the world in which the operations of Mr. Chamberlain would meet with success, if it be not superfluous to detail specific territories in face of the abundant evidence of general success which this horoscope affords.

Friends and Enemies

It was the boast of Bismarck that he was the "best-hated man in Europe," and it would be strange indeed if Mr. Chamberlain had passed through life and attained so prominent a position without incurring the enmity or arousing the envy and malice of a considerable number of individuals. Nevertheless, there are only two aspects in this horoscope which seem to point to any sort of trouble from such causes. The points are those of Neptune, which afflicts both the Moon and Venus, and of Mars which afflicts Uranus in the Midheaven and the Sun in the 2nd House.

By referring these two points to the Ecliptic we find they correspond to the Sun's position on or about the 24th of May, and the 26th of January, and I shall leave the reader to look up his Almanac and find the individuals (illustrious they must needs be to find chronicle in Whittaker) who were capable of filling the requirements of the case.

As to friends, Mr. Chamberlain should lack nothing. With the Moon in sextile to the Sun and Jupiter, the ruler of the 11th House, in the same benefic relations with the Moon, he would always be able to count upon a strong adherence, and the only adverse indication in this matter is that Mars, part ruler of the 11th House, holds the 12th House in square aspect to Uranus in the Midheaven. This would be interpreted to mean that some of his friends will be disposed to become his enemies, and to militate, although ineffectually, against his credit and position. Why ineffectually? Because Mercury, the ruler of the Ascendant and prime significator of Mr. Chamberlain, is angular and well aspected, while Mars is weak and afflicted by Uranus which is in elevation above it.

A Popular Illustration

Conclusion

Let it not be thought that the fame and position which Mr. Chamberlain has attained in the political world is due entirely to the benefic position of the principal planets in his horoscope of birth. Opportunity is not everything. The ability to use it counts for much, and only a man of exceptional industry, firmness, and decision, could have won for himself such peculiar distinction; and only a man of singular faculty could have sustained his position in the face of so much determined opposition. It will doubtless be a matter of extreme interest to the student of this horoscope, as to every one interested in the political situation of to-day, to observe the concurrent influences at work in the year 1904-5. Mr. Chamberlain attained his sixty-eighth birthday anniversary on the 8th of July, 1904, and by adding that number of degrees to the 22nd degree of Aquarius we obtain Taurus 0 as the point which has attained the meridian by "direction." This is called the Progressed Midheaven. Referring this point of the Zodiac to the places of the planets at birth, it is observed that the Midheaven is approaching the sextile aspect of Mercury, having recently passed the opposition of Saturn, and having attained that aspect in 1905, it passes in 1908 to the sextile of Uranus, the planet which holds the greatest elevation in the horoscope of birth. The Ascendant under the Midheaven of Taurus 0 is Leo 16° 28′, which is the Progressed Ascendant for the year 1904. It is in semisquare aspect to Mercury, and is the occasion of many anxieties, worries, and annoyances,

Astrology

and some journeys by water. It also indicates some derangement of the health due to nervous strain, and affecting the stomach (ruled by Cancer). The Sun is directed in similar manner to the 24th degree of the sign Virgo, where it meets the sextile aspect of Jupiter in the 2nd House, in the sign of its exaltation, Cancer. This gives access of good fortune, increase of honor and prestige, and as Jupiter rules the 11th House, many adherents and supporters. But being also in semisquare to Venus, Mr. Chamberlain is in danger of losing a brother or other near male relative. The Moon by the same measure is within 4 degrees of the place of Jupiter, again marking the year 1908 as one of exceptional advantage, and in July of that year Jupiter passes over the Progressed Ascendant.

During the year 1904 Saturn has been close to the Midheaven of the radical horoscope, being in Aquarius 21, and stationary therein, during the month of June. In March, and again in October, it transits the opposition of the Progressed Ascendant in Aquarius 16, while in February, June, and December Uranus is in transit over the opposition of the radical Ascendant in Sagittarius 28° 16′.

In 1905, Saturn will transit the Midheaven in the horoscope of birth, and in the summer of the same year Mars will be Stationary in opposition to the place of the Moon at birth. Both these periods will be fraught with cares and anxieties, and the latter influence will act detrimentally on the health, disposing to attacks of gout and inflammatory action in the system.

But while the approaching and concurrent Primary directions are of a highly benefic nature, there will be no hint of a breakdown either in health or reputation, and

A Popular Illustration

it needs only the additional good influence of a transit or Secondary Lunar direction to carry Mr. Chamberlain at full swing to the summit of popular esteem and political power.

The curious who seek for coincidences will not be surprised and may be gratified to note that Merx, the root of the name of Mercury, signifies trade, and that the planet Mercury is rising in this horoscope of Mr. Chamberlain, who won great distinction for himself as President of the Board of Trade. Those who in more earnest vein seek for causes will do well to trace the transits of the major planets through this horoscope over the places of the Significators, the Sun, Moon, Midheaven, and Ascendant at all the important epochs in the life of the late Colonial Secretary. The working out of the more important directional arcs for the same period I can safely leave to the reader whose desire to thoroughly test the claims of Astrology has been sufficiently aroused by the perusal of these pages. It is at all times easier to dispute than to disprove, and this apparently is the reason for so much that is said, and so little that is shown, against Astrology.

As to the *modus operandi* of planetary influence I conceive that the brain cells are infilled with a nervous pabulum of such delicate nature as to be capable of responding to the finer etheric vibrations instituted by the planets; that the electrostatic condition of the earth's atmosphere at the moment of birth determines the particular mode or modes of vibration to which the individual brain is syntonically responsive; and I could, did space permit, immediately adduce hundreds of instances to show that whenever the same positions or planetary

Astrology

aspects recur in the heavens as were in existence at the moment of a birth, the individual immediately responds to the excitation, and gives instant evidence of such excitation by actions in agreement with the nature of the planets involved.